I0802261

Five North American Architects
An Anthology by Kenneth Frampton

Five North American Architects

An Anthology by Kenneth Frampton

Stanley Saitowitz
Brigitte Shim + Howard Sutcliffe
Rick Joy
John + Patricia Patkau
Steven Holl

Columbia University GSAPP
Lars Müller Publishers

Kenneth Frampton

Kenneth Frampton is the Ware Professor of Architecture at the Graduate School of Architecture, Planning, and Preservation, Columbia University and has served as a member of its faculty since 1973. He was born in the United Kingdom in 1930 and graduated as an architect from the Architectural Association, London, in 1956. Before migrating to the United States in 1965 to teach at Princeton University he was an associate in the practice of Douglas Stephen & Partners, London, while simultaneously serving as technical editor of the magazine *Architectural Design*. From 1976–1980 he was a Fellow of the Institute of Architecture and Urban Studies, New York, where he also served as a founding editor of the magazine *Oppositions*. Among his publications is the study *Modern Architecture: A Critical History,* first published in 1980. Since coming to the US, he has been mostly involved in teaching and writing.

Architecture and Continuity: North American Architecture 1990–2010

Kenneth Frampton

The ambiguity which truly matters, the sense-giving ambivalence, the genuine foundation on which the cognitive usefulness of conceiving human habitat as the "world of culture" rests, is the ambivalence between "creativity" and "normative regulation." The two ideas could not be further apart, yet both are–and must remain–present in the composite idea of culture. "Culture" is as much about inventing as it is about preserving; about discontinuity as much as about continuation; about novelty as much as about tradition; about routine as much as about pattern-breaking; about norm-following as much as about the transcendence of norm; about the unique as much as about the regular; about change as much as about monotony of reproduction; about the unexpected as much as about the predictable.

Zygmunt Bauman, *Culture as Praxis,* 1999

I wish to express my gratitude to Dean Mark Wigley for having invited me to curate an event in honor of my 80th birthday. I believe that he envisaged me asking a number of scholars to deliver papers in accordance with the *Festschrift* tradition, but instead I felt I should use the occasion to present something of the current state of architecture as a practice rather than once more privileging theory. To this end, I opted to invite five distinguished architectural offices to present their work so as to constitute the basis for a mutual reflection upon the status of architectural culture in North America today. As is evident from the work of these five practices who graciously accepted to participate, I elected to construe the rubric of North America to include Canada as well as the United States. In this regard, I wanted to draw attention not only to the exceptional quality of recent architecture in the U.S., but also to work of comparable caliber in Canada; a fact which contemporary critical opinion still somehow manages to ignore. Hence this somewhat unusual combination of Canadian and American work represents something of a polemic against the habitual provinciality of the center.

All anthologies are somewhat invidious, and a preposterously partial one such as this, comprising only five offices, is bound to be even more so. Thus, I beg the indulgence of those distinguished American and Canadian architects who were not selected to participate in this event.

Within the U.S., I elected to focus on the work of three offices that may be said to represent a phenomenological approach to architecture within the States. To this end, I chose two established practices, representative of the West and East Coasts; namely, Stanley Saitowitz and Steven Holl, plus a third figure, Rick Joy, currently practicing in the American Southwest in Tucson, and who may be seen as occupying an intermediate position. As far as Canada is concerned, I chose to highlight the work of two offices: Patkau Architects of Vancouver and Shim-Sutcliffe Architects, based in Toronto, that is to say, architects from the Canadian Northwest and Midwest respectively. This selection unfortunately meant excluding the rich contemporary architectural culture of Québec and the Maritimes.

Despite its arbitrary character, this selection was not determined solely on the basis of location, despite my bias towards representing practices from the north. Thus, apart from the subjectivity of personal taste, the choice was largely determined by the presence of certain tectonic values and by a concomitant preoccupation with a poetic of materials that may be found to some degree in all five practices. Another prominent common factor is the importance that each of these practices gives to the topographic character of the site. At the risk of oversimplifying, I would like to suggest that despite fundamental differences, all of these practices manifest a common concern for emphasizing the following expressive tropes, as these may be found throughout their work; namely, *landscape, material, structure, craft, space,* and *light*.

Although one may contend that many of these modes are invariably present in almost all works of architecture, I would like to suggest that this is far from being the case in today's all too worldly architectural production. Instead, we often encounter a prevalence of spectacular sculptural effects that, in the end, manifest little concern for the topography within which they are situated. Even more frequently, we are confronted with buildings in which everything is given over to the tactile aesthetics of the exterior finish rather than to any significant articulation of the inner volume. Likewise, structural elements may be used in such a profligate and illogical manner as to border on the unethical. Instead of indulging in such superficial, ostentatious effects, all of the practices assembled here are committed to integrating their works within the given context in nuanced ways. And while they are all preoccupied with material expression, they do not pursue this mode at the expense of according sufficient attention to the rhythmic articulation of both form and volume. Finally, the presence of refined craft and the iterative articulation of light are two interrelated aspects that are present in every one of these practices to varying degrees. By craft, I mean in the first instance the craft of architecture as a practice in itself, what Herman Hertzberger once referred to as "the skill of an architect," as though architecture, in the last analysis, is a trade that one had to master if one was going to imagine and synthesize and articulate a complex whole with any assurance. Thus despite the unavoidable presence of digital procedures and processes, this last implies a conscious cultivation of craft within the studio and on site, wherein manual technique, rationalized by technology, still obtains as a guarantor of quality in architecture.

This brings me to the most elusive attribute of all, namely, the varying quality of light, which, while constantly modulated by the climate, the hour and the season, nonetheless provides a certain luminosity that not only varies from one place to the next, but also from one building to the next. It is possibly the most ineffable phenomenon engendered by architecture; one that is often correctly perceived as being inseparable from the aura of a building. One may think of it as a fluctuating essence within a given work arising out of the interplay between topography, structure, space, craft, and material.

There remains in all of these practices one other crucial attribute, namely, their propensity for typological invention, whereby the building becomes a vehicle for the realization of a certain specific program; one that is never fully available until the occupation of the work. What I have in mind can perhaps only be clarified by citing certain works for the way in which both program and form come together to transcend their separate genesis as in, say, the large overhanging roof of the Gleneagles Community Center in West Vancouver designed by Patkau Architects, which apart from its climatological function embodies and symbolizes the tectonic status of the work with respect to the community. Something tectonically symbolic also occurs in the case of Holl's School of Art and Art History, University of Iowa (2006), wherein a neo-cubist structural composition is able to imply the interdisciplinary affinities between the two fields it accommodates while at the same time celebrating the unique topography over which its structure is dynamically suspended.

Something equally responsive to the context, typologically as well as topographically, is evident in Saitowitz's remarkable structure for the Yerba Buena Lofts (2002), conceived as though it were a typological condensation of Le Corbusier's *bloc à cellules.* What is immediately striking in this instance is the way in which the repetitive modular order of the duplex lofts serves to reiterate the rhythm of the traditional low-rise residential fabric of the city. It proffers a new form of urban living while simultaneously demonstrating how compact, narrow-fronted studio units may be ingeniously combined around a rectangular parking garage while being aggregated into a rhythmically compelling mass form, while achieving the tight economy of its orthogonal assembly and the precision of its cross-wall concrete constructional system. At the same time, the spatially different life styles afforded by the units has been brilliantly achieved through a varied range of alternative types. The overall typo-morpho result is that the building sits within the area south of Market Street in San Francisco as a *répétition différente* that looks as if it has always been there.

A typo-topographical invention of equal brilliance and of comparable representational authority is evident in the so-called Integral House (2009), built to the designs of Shim-Sutcliffe architects, on a shallow escarpment overlooking a shallow ravine to the north of downtown Toronto. What makes this work unique is the way in which its organic plan-form seems to have been inspired as much by the meander of a stream flowing through the flat bottom of the ravine as by the contours of the wooded slope upon which the house is subtly poised. In a typical metaphorical-formal overlay of which only architects of exceptional sensibility are capable, the organic plan/sectional configuration of the principal space also pertains to the doubly articulated public/private articulation of the house as a whole, for while it remains, in the last analysis, a large luxurious residence for a highly cultivated bachelor, in its broader public aspect, it is nothing less than an exceptional generous civic space for the public performance of chamber music and discreet theatrical pieces.

Rick Joy's work in the Sonoran desert outside of Tucson is equally a series of excursions into the poetic potential of topographic form, re-presenting, in this instance, the empathetic expansiveness that may be experienced by the individual subject before the exotic, untamed, oceanic expanse of the desert, curtailed only by an infinitely distant range of mountains. Both the Tyler House, Tubac (2001) and the Desert Nomad House near Tucson (2005) establish a domestic space of appearance before the enigmatic undulating of the desert, with its exotic flora and fauna. In each instance the siting and orientation derives from the inflection and concatenation of the rock-strewn scrub, as it falls away across a middle ground towards a distant mountainous vista. In both houses, it is the Cor-Ten clad, rusting image of the house without and the framed panorama of the landscape within that jointly make for the sharply poetic character of the whole. One should not forget to note with regard to Joy's practice to date that in the case of the Amangiri Resort in Utah he collaborated with two other architects Wendell Burnette of Phoenix and Marwan Al Sayed currently practicing out of Los Angeles.

Among all the architects included in this anthology, Patkau Architects of Vancouver are surely the most tectonically attuned for the way in which they establish a reciprocity between the topography of the site and the articulation of the structure. This is never more evident than in their Strawberry Vale School, Victoria, British Columbia (1995) or in their very different Grande Bibliothèque de Québec, Montreal (2005). In the first instance, we have an organic plan broken up into cheveroned clusters of classrooms with mono-pitched roofs sloping gently away from the central vertebrae of the building. These roofs project out into a micro-landscape made up of moss-laden rocks running parallel to the southern face of the building. In the second, the Québec library, we are confronted by a ship-like form carefully integrated into the grain of the city and faced in horizontal green glass planks. An altogether different topographical tack is taken in the long box-framed profile of their recently completed Linear House (2009), running parallel to a line of fir trees that divide a preexisting farm into two different domains: the one partially domestic in character and the other still fully agrarian. In this way the house derives as much from the existing structure and use of the site as it does from a specific elaboration of the program.

Like the Patkau schools Steven Holl's academic buildings are among his finest along with the truly remarkable museums that he has to his credit, including the Kiasma Museum of Contemporary Art in Helsinki (1998) through to the Nelson-Atkins Museum of Art Extension in Kansas City, Missouri (2004). Despite its partly subterranean character, this last is a tour de force in luminosity. In this museum the optimum nineteenth-century gallery section, favoring indirect top light, is adapted so as to yield a seemingly random sequence of five, irregularly shaped, galleries of varying size and shape, clad with opaque channel glass. These giant lanterns, glowing at night with artificial light and suffused with natural light during the day, not only provide zenithal light but also serve to air-condition the space through that which Holl calls "breathing T's," a term deriving from their sectional form.

In a certain sense Holl may be seen as a veteran within this anthology for although the other four practices have not been directly influenced by him, his work nonetheless evokes the phenomenological values to which they variously aspire. And there is also, here and there, common typological points of departure, as in the trope of the stepped reading room, which first appeared in Holl's 1988 competition entry for the Amerika Gedenk Bibliothek in Berlin, and which now emerges somewhat uncannily as an honorific reading room form in the libraries Patkau Architects, in its Grande Bibliothèque du Québec designed in 2000, and then in the Winnipeg Central Library Addition designed in 2002. And it is this trope, so far unrealized by Holl, that forms the core of his Queens Library as it is currently projected for a site next to the famous Pepsi-Cola sign in Queens.

It may be that such a stepped section does not contribute in a fundamental way to the performative aspects of the reading room as a type and that such symbolic space-forms are at variance with the task of mediating the environmental challenges currently facing society. While not subscribing to the total autonomy of architectural form, it has to be acknowledged that architecture does have its practical and expressive limits; and yet, at the same time, it is a cultural manifestation inextricably enmeshed with the lifeworld and as such, able to offset the commodifying conditions universally prevailing in the megalopoli of today's regional urbanization.

Much of the work in this anthology displays a penchant for certain tactile effects, so much so that one is tempted to posit the presence of a common palette, wherein there is a mutual inclination toward certain material, resources, and effects. I have in mind the prevalence in much of this work of Cor-Ten steel, channel glass, perforated metal, precisely milled timber, in various incarnations, and the drive to achieve equally precise results in cast-in-place and precast concrete elements via meticulous vibration techniques and equally precise formwork in timber or steel. This common tactile materiality invariably extends to the landscape wherein a similar common approach obtains towards the integration of water and plant material along with the concomitant layering and manipulation of the earth's surface. There is a key, crucial awareness in much of this work of the sensuous/acoustical experience of the body-being, as it transverses the transition through the polarities of entry versus ascent, hard versus soft, and dark versus light.

An indicator of this common sensibility was evident in the looped flat-screen presentations that provided a comprehensive overview of the work of the five firms, as these were set up side-by-side in the foyer of Wood Auditorium where the symposium was held. Although I was already aware of affinities between these practices, I had not expected this juxtaposition to yield such a hallucinating spectrum in which the random conjunction of two adjacent images from different offices would seem momentarily, at times, to have come from the same hand, or at the very least, to be evidence of the spontaneous existence of a single "school."

I cannot possibly pretend that my selection of these architects has not been influenced by my preoccupation with the concept of critical regionalism as this was first formulated by Alex Tzonis and Liane Lefaivre in their 1981 essay "The Grid and Pathway."[1] This insightful yet cautious take on the legacy of the Greek modernist tradition involved a mode of beholding that would be further elaborated by me in an 1983 essay entitled "Towards A Critical Regionalism: Six Points for an Architecture of Resistance."[2] While this is not the place to reiterate this argument or to impose such a reading on any of the architects represented here, it would be disingenuous of me not to acknowledge the way in which this paradigm continues to influence my overview of contemporary architecture. In any case, it is clear from the substance which follows, that in addition to their penchant for typological invention, all of these architects have habitually assumed a highly contextual approach to the creation of architecture.

Against this background it is pertinent to state that had this been a larger anthology I would have included a number of other North American architects whose work seems to me to be particularly sensitive and of relevance to our current historical situation. It should be also acknowledged that if one were to be strict about the geographical extent of the North American continent, one would also have to include a number of Mexican architects who would necessarily take their proper place within a more comprehensive overview.[3] Finally, one cannot entirely deny the arbitrariness of only electing to represent five practices, this being due to the fact that the symposium had to be completed in the space of a single day.

Otherwise this is the record of a rich and intense event in which the presentations of the five architectural offices followed each other in a fairly rapid succession to culminate at the end of the day in a relatively brief and at times contentious discussion between the architects, the audience, and myself.

1 Alex Tzonis and Liane Lefaivre, "The Grid and the Pathway: An Introduction to the Work of Dimitris and Suzana Antonakakis," *Architecture in Greece* (1981) p. 164–78
2 Kenneth Frampton, "Towards a Critical Regionalism: Six Points for an Architecture of Resistance," in *The Anti-Aesthetic. Essays on Postmodern Culture,* edited by Hal Foster (Seattle: Bay Press, 1983), p. 16–30.
3 Among others, such figures as José Aldrete-Haas, Augusto Alvarez, Albert Kalach, Ricardo Legorreta, Antonio Toca Fernandez, and Abraham Zabludovsky.

Poster designed by Willi Kunz announcing the symposium "Five Architects: A North American Anthology," held at the Graduate School of Architecture, Planning and Preservation, Columbia University, November 13, 2010

Stanley Saitowitz

Stanley Saitowitz is the principal of Stanley Saitowitz | Natoma Architects, Inc., San Francisco. He was born in Johannesburg, South Africa in 1949 and received his Bachelor of Architecture from the University of the Witwatersrand, Johannesburg in 1975, and his Master of Architecture from the University of California, Berkeley in 1977.

Saitowitz has received numerous awards, including AIA San Francisco and AIA Tampa Bay Awards in 2010 for the Tampa Museum of Art, the Kirby Ward Fitzpatrick Prize for the Best New Building in San Francisco for his Beth Sholom synagogue in 2008, and the AIA Best of the Bay Award in three consecutive years, 2003, 2004, and 2005, for the Yerba Buena Lofts, the Lieff Residence, and Beth Sholom Synagogue.

Emeritus Professor of Architecture at the University of California, Berkeley, Saitowitz has taught at a number of schools, including the Graduate School of Design, Harvard University (Eliot Noyes Professor 1991–92), University of Oklahoma (Bruce Goff Professor, 1993), Southern California Institute of Architecture, UCLA, University of Texas, the University of the Witwatersrand, and Cornell and Syracuse universities.

Stanley Saitowitz
Simplicity and Synthesis

I am thankful, firstly for being here for a milestone in the life of a person I greatly admire. I am also grateful to Ken for his many years of serving as a rudder, so to speak, for his helping to steer architecture. Since I left school and began working, his values have directed my efforts and helped me continue with an architectural agenda, weathering the tangents and the fads that have emerged over time. His voice and the work he has upheld have been a continuous source of aspiration and inspiration. It is hard to imagine what my own work would be today without the concepts Ken has crystallized over the years. His 1969 article in Perspecta 12—presenting the Maison de Verre as a building in time rather than as an object—totally changed the way I thought about architecture.

While I was still a student in Johannesburg, Alison and Peter Smithson visited and shared their particular sense of English modernism, mentioning the idea of a "Veld parallel." That visit set me on a path that I later transplanted to San Francisco, a path that I was only able to name after Ken's writings on critical regionalism appeared. This continues to be the direction of my work. Both schools that I attended stopped teaching history before the last chapter of Sir Banister Fletcher's *A History of Architecture on the Comparative Method* and as a result there was no comprehensive account of the work that interested me most until Frampton's *Modern Architecture: A Critical History* appeared in 1980. That book was on every reading list that I ever made at the University of California, Berkeley. *Studies in Tectonic Culture* was the final nail in the coffin of postmodernism. Each of these, to name only the most obvious, is pivotal to my work.

The word "practice" is derived from the Greek "pragma," meaning action. The theory that drives my practice is pragmatism derived from the same root. Pragmatism, originated in the United States in the 1870s and has always represented a distinctly American way of thinking. Pragmatists argue that the function of philosophy should be to find out what definite difference it makes to our lives. Beliefs are rules for action; to develop a thought's meaning, we need to determine what it produces. Pragmatism does not have rigid canons or abstract dogmas. It unstiffens theories, is genial, and entertains any hypothesis that has practical consequences. We develop a set of principles for each project derived from the particular situation and specific site. I will present three.

View of San Francisco and the Golden Gate Bridge under fog

Typical San Francisco street lined with row houses

The first things I learned about San Francisco were from songs, long before I moved there. Working in a city of songs and being part of building this city has been my focus. I have constantly searched to understand its nature, something Ambrose Bierce captured when he wrote, "This city is a point upon a map of fog." There are 179,000 building parcels in San Francisco of which 173,000 or 87.8 percent are residential. Housing is by far the most important constituent element of the fabric of this city. Naturally this has been central to our work.

The first attempt to deal with the Victorian row house typology was our office loft, built in 1991. This was followed by a number of other buildings in which we developed prototypes and as well as a particular approach to urban housing. Fifteen years later we built the building next door and later, another one, a few of blocks away. Then we had the opportunity to realize a whole streetscape with the commission for the Yerba Buena Lofts.

Stanley Saitowitz | Natoma Architects Office, San Francisco, 1991

Yerba Buena Lofts
San Francisco, California, 2002

I have always been interested in continuity of built form that is more than form itself. The subdivision and redivision of land, the grids within grids, which can be understood right down to the scale of a building's individual units and eventually even to its furniture, are the ordering devices of this city. At Yerba Buena Lofts this urban logic is extruded vertically to become the structure of the building. Each loft is thought of as a stacked plot and the building is a rigorous and repetitive subdivision of plots.

Our urban housing emerges from highly modulated and systematic plans. We use the lessons of mass production and although there are claims that current technologies will bypass the need for identically repeated elements, we use the economies of serialization to increase quality. We never had an interest in arbitrary variety, preferring to make all units the same and good and when inhabited, the neutral spaces we provide result in much more variety than I, as the architect, could ever imagine.

I have always wondered if our architecture could be a tool of liberation. Very early I began to confront the question of indeterminacy versus programming, smooth versus striated space. The first building I built outside Johannesburg in 1976 was an artist's loft. It was conceived as a scaffold—a frame to make a painting in. It followed two precedents—Pierre Chareau and Bernard Bijvoet's Maison de Verre (1932) and Charles and Ray Eames's House in Santa Monica (1949). I thought of it as an instrument rather than an object, more like a telephone than a conversation, more like a camera than a photograph. I was so intent on destroying the program that I refused to have a bathroom. A toilet floated behind a court on one level, a tub was set on another, a shower was placed on yet another. The dining room was a mobile cart, which rolled around the house and out into the garden through the hangar doors.

In our current housing, in order to provide indeterminate deprogrammed space, kitchens and bathrooms are cumulative, collapsed, and minimized. These servant programs are compressed into thick end walls, eliminating the whole idea of rooms and replacing them with minimally differentiated continuous fields. The plans consist of thickened walls and open space. The service walls double as structure and align vertically stacked plumbing. All electrical and sprinkler lines run in chase through these zones, producing added economies. All lighting emanates from these dense walls.

This process of reduction, compression, and repetition provides opportunities for expansion and the reallocation of resources to increase qualities in other areas. Through hierarchical unities, elements are assembled, grouped and minimized, providing the maximum amount of free space for the occupants to determine their own program.

With the Case Study Houses of the 1950s, a new image of modern dwelling emerged in California. Spacious, open, and free, it redefined the domestic landscape as a fluid and continuous field. This house fully embraced the mechanisms and appliances

of modern life, placing them with the same ease as the furniture was placed. We have used this dwelling model for the design of our multi-family housing. Density and intensity have their own demands and the projects we do are the result.

The lowest level of the Yerba Buena Lofts has living-cum-work space units for artists that were stipulated as a part of the regulations for developing the building. Zoning established this use to provide affordable incubator space for art-related activities. Above those are the stacked units with recesses in the facade, which is a code requirement established to prevent large buildings from being built in San Francisco. There is also a sense of the building as a continuous extrusion of the structure and fabric of the city, the texture of which gets replicated in the building itself. The building bridges two zones of the city. From a height of 85 feet (25.9 m), it steps down to 40 feet (12.2 m), which is the average of the southern part of the site.

The main lobby and the entry to the parking garage are buried within the center of the building and another set of lofts with garden units connect the alleyway to a second, smaller entry lobby. The parking is contained within the doughnut of units and I realized that the ability to drive in and park at your kitchen was very marketable as part of the American dream.

The street wall is composed of of bays and balconies, which articulate the edge as it meets the city. The podium connects to the 40-foot height of the zone behind with the same treatment along its edges, demarcating the beginning of the upper part of the building, where it begins to step back, establishing different unit types.

HEALTHCARE
974-5611

Yerba Buena Lofts, San Francisco, CA, 2002. View of north-facing facade along Folsom Street

The typical articulation of the edge condition has inset balconies, as well as channel glass on the outer limit facing the street. Inside there is clear glass, which provides a private court just behind the facade. The translucent, horizontal glazing creates a sense of privacy and the clear glass section creates outdoor space The result is that every unit has its own private outdoor space, and some of the units on top of the podium have large garden terraces.

The project is an example of counter-contextualism; the horizontal channeled glass replicates something of the clapboard siding found in San Francisco and the rhythm of the typical domestic parcel is picked up in the iteration of the bays. The contextualism works both ways. The organizational structure of the vertical lots has a 16-by-16 foot (4.9 × 4.9 m) space in which the bay, the balcony, and the house are created. There is a fairly random variation to produce a rich urban texture. At night the spaces behind the channel glass take on the appearance of lanterns, creating a degree of variety out of a very simple system. The images, which start to emerge, are reminiscent of some Victorian version of a city of towers.

The key to this building's competitive price in the marketplace was actually in the highly repetitive construction system used. Basically the same formwork was used all the way up, sliding forms that were inserted and pulled up. The production of the building is also its completion. After the concrete has cured, the glass is inserted and at that point the building is finished and water proofed. In comparable buildings being built in San Francisco using similar techniques of construction, seven trades follow each other to create the seal; the concrete is hidden between the framing skin, window inserts, flashing, and a final rain screen.

In this case only two trades were needed to achieve the completion. The building is built from within itself, which meant that it did not need any scaffolding and little actual work was done on the exterior. These savings were translated into using better materials. In competitive buildings, it is usually impossible to get the amount of glass as we used here for virtually the entire facade of the building is constructed of glass. As the building was being still being poured it was possible to finish the lower units. Thus work went on continuously, compressing the time frame, which is a huge economy. By the time the roof was being constructed, the building had already been sealed up and was being completed in the interior.

The structural concrete used throughout the building is as cast but we did some tuning up. We saw-cut the structural slab at grade and stained it to produce a finish for the lobby. The 8-by-8 foot (2.4 m) cubes are articulated at each doorstep with color that announces the front doors. Four sub-types for each unit are created by the require-ment to set back parts of the facade. The units were produced as a raw shell. With urban housing, it is the cubic dimension rather than the square footage that is a measure of the generosity of the building. There was also an option of purchasing one's finishes. This led to an enormous variation of units. I have been in many of the 200 units in the building and they are almost all distinguishable from one another by virtue of the simple principle of allowing people to choose their own final finishes according to their taste.

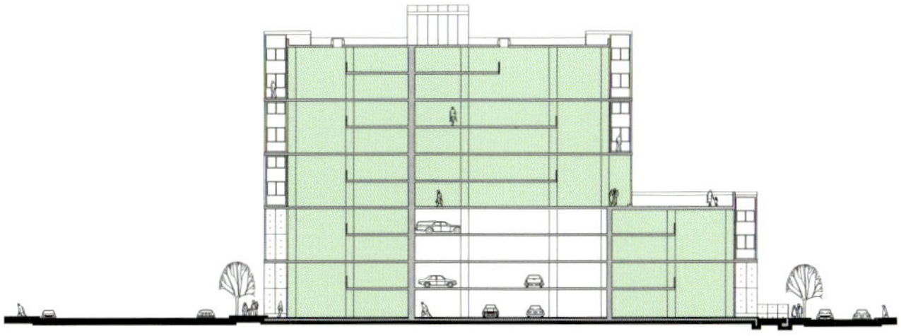

Cross section

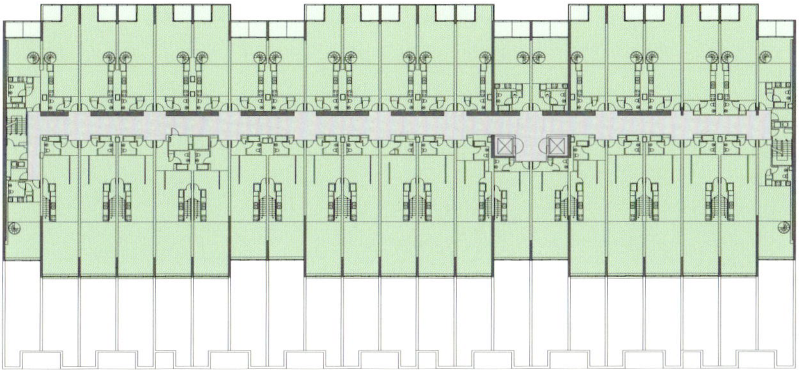

Plan above the fourth floor

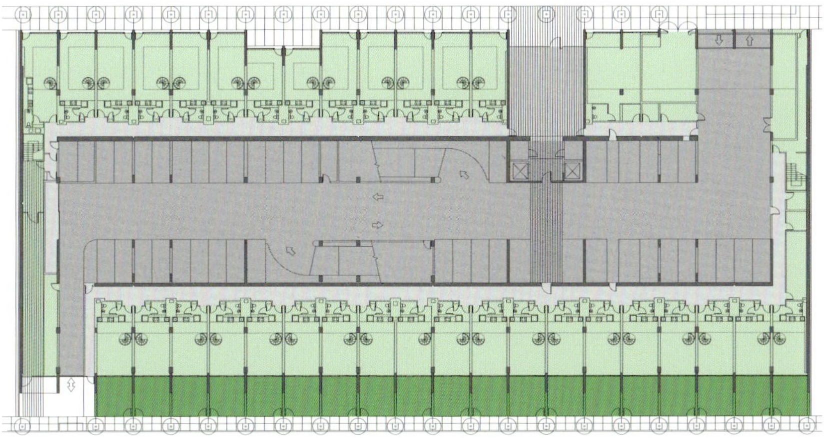

Plan below the fourth floor

0 5 10 20

Yerba Buena Lofts, Typical cross section and plans

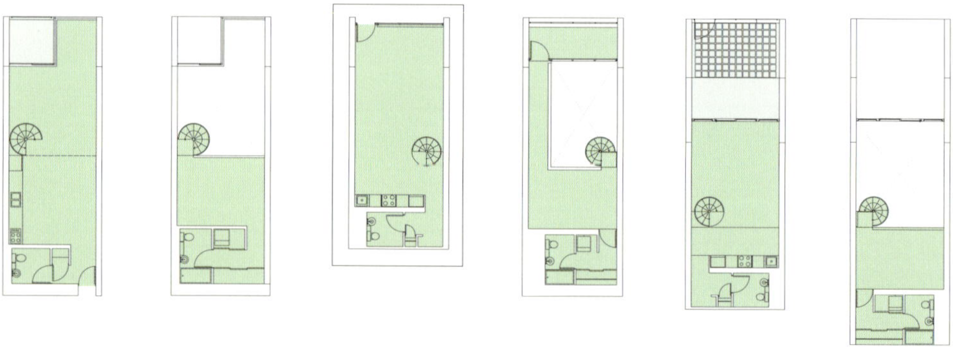

Yerba Buena Lofts. Typical double-height unit plans

Detail view at night

Typical mezzanine bedroom level

Main pedestrian entrance

Yerba Buena Lofts. Close-up of building under construction

General view of building at twilight

Tampa Museum of Art
Tampa, Florida, 2010

Museums began in ancient times as temples dedicated to the muses where the privileged went to witness beauty and to learn. After the Renaissance, museums became monumental through the provision of palatial structures and the idea of the gallery arose as a space to display paintings and sculpture. Later, museums became centers of education and research, collecting and actively provoking the exchange of ideas. By presenting the highest achievements of culture, museums became a stabilizing and regenerative force, crusading for quality and excellence. The role of the modern museum is both aesthetic and didactic—both temple and forum.

The design of contemporary museums can be characterized by two polar approaches. On one hand, there is an approach in which the building aims to be a work of art itself, an independent sculptural object. On the other hand there are museums designed to act as neutral containers, to serve as beautiful treasure chests whose sole purpose is to be filled with art.

This museum is a neutral frame for the display of art, an empty canvas to be filled with paintings. It is a blank container, a scaffold and infrastructure to be completed by its contents. The building floats in the park, embracing it through its overhanging shelter and reflective walls. It is a hovering abstraction gliding above the ground.

The site brought some complicated conditions. No art program could be located within the floodplain, and the site is located in area with an 18-foot (5.5 m) high-water level. It is a part of a reconstruction program for the downtown of Tampa, along with the famous Kiley Gardens, which have fallen into disrepair, and the arresting form of a cylindrical office tower designed by Harry Wolf. Tampa is a suburban city and for this reason we attempted to create a cultural center with a new park, a children's museum, and the Tampa Museum of Art.

The program on the ground is all non-art related, except for the delivery and handling of artworks. The program begins on the riverside with a bookstore and cafe, along with a large multi-purpose lobby and some meeting rooms. The building is clearly divided into two zones, one containing all the public programs relating to the art and its display, and the other accommodating the extensive support programs. Each of these zones is organized around a court. The court of the galleries is a pivot affording a clear itinerary by which to experience all the gallery spaces. The support building is organized around another court in the rear. These courtyards help to consolidate the programs of the two separate buildings, which are joined by a gap. A massive cantilever produces a shade-creating public porch. When I went to the site for the first time, it was so hot that I had to go back to my hotel and wait for the sun to go down. I decided immediately that one had to create shade out of the building. The program actually facilitated such an approach.

The structure that supports the massive 40-foot (12.2 m) cantilever is a series of shear cores with girders attached from which the cantilever hangs. One of the essential activities of a museum is its collection, and this always creates the need for expansion.

Tampa Museum of Art, Tampa, FL, 2010.
Detail of the cantilevered mass-form above the promenade

It was really important to establish a system that would provide the possibility of growth. One could read the project a mat building, with a grid of cores establishing a certain set of building blocks, from which the museum can perpetuate itself.

One of the big problems of the project, however, was that the museum currently has a minimal collection. It is more like a Kunsthalle, and many of its exhibitions are borrowed. In addition, very strict insurance requirements allow for no daylight in the galleries. We had this blank object and no real architectural context to work with. So I chose the sky and the water to be the elements to think about in terms of how to enrich the exterior quality of the container, and to make an object that was without content or image, but which would have a changing, shimmering life, not unlike nature itself.

The museum was realized on an incredibly modest budget, and we had to really beg for money. It was finally built for under $400 a square foot (ca. $4,300 a square meter), which is much less than some of our custom-made houses. We achieved this through perforated metal panels produced by McNichols, a company that operates out of Tampa. These perforated panels were separated by six inches (15 cm) and slightly offset, so as to introduce a moiré pattern that causes the building to flicker and to reconfigure its surface constantly.

The entry lobby is integrated with the approach from the town along the pathway underneath the porch toward the river. One walks down a quiet space and ends up right near the water before entering. There is a sculpture court as part of the gallery space above. The idea is that the museum should always operate as a frame.

The main entry lobby is made entirely out of glass and the two ends, running parallel to the river, are left completely open. The space flows through and links to other cultural institutions like the Performing Arts Center and the University of Tampa. The galleries were intended to be as neutral as possible. The white polished concrete and parasol fabric of the ceiling overcome the problem of not having any daylight. To this end we attempted to create a day sky with artificial light.

Tampa Museum of Art. View from the river

Detail of the rain screen wall and separation between the exhibition and storage wings of the museum

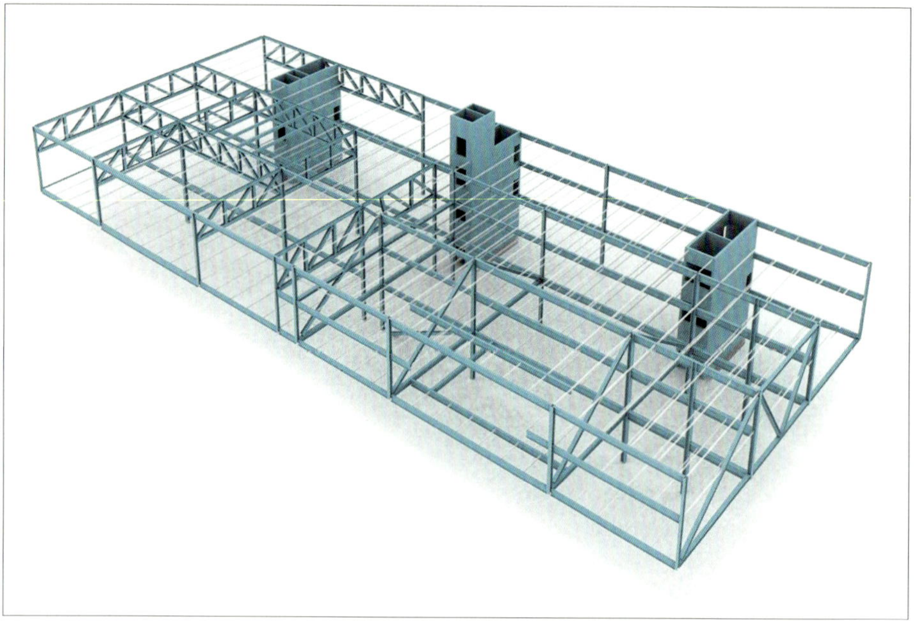

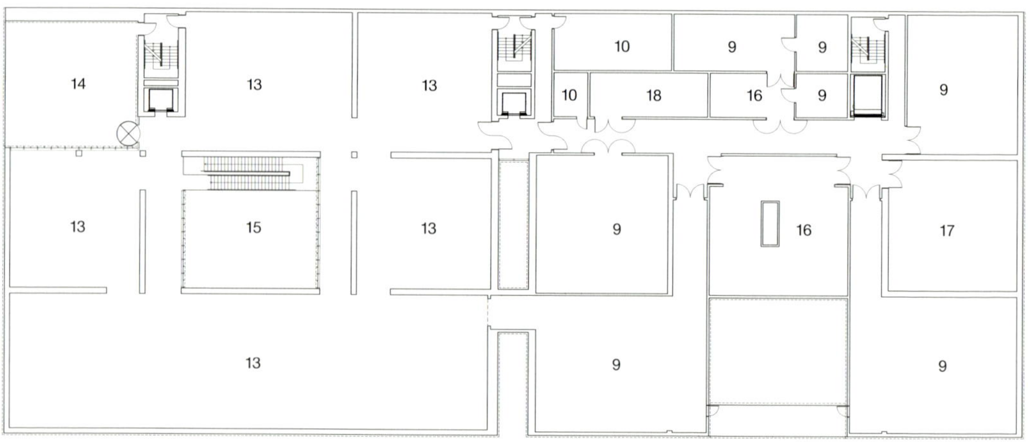

Second floor

1 Lobby And Reception
2 Ticket Desk
3 Museum Store
4 Museum Cafe
5 Conference Room
6 Classroom
7 Restroom
8 Catering Kitchen
9 Storage
10 Maintenance
11 Loading Dock
12 Security
13 Gallery
14 Balcony
15 Atrium
16 Workshop
17 Staging
18 Registrar

0 5 10

Tampa Museum of Art. Isometric of the steel frame and service cores

Plan of main floor

View through the “window” in the storage wing over the park and the riverfront

Tampa Museum of Art. View of LED-floodlit wall at night

All of the mechanisms are held as high above the ceiling as possible in order to keep the spaces neutral. To enable the moiré patterns to reveal themselves at night we arranged for a series of LED lights in the gap between the two skins. This presents the image of a museum that virtually turns itself inside out at night and becomes a big urban canvas. Artists have been hired to create various artworks on this surface. The museum is a live urban porch at night, a jewel box floating on a glass pedestal, hovering in the park as a hyphen between ground and sky.

Seven Principles of Architecture

I wanted to end with my seven principles of architecture.

1. Each building begins with a site and the particular desire to transform it. Buildings are made of matter, and a continuation of the geological processes that produce their sites as part of a natural evolution. A building marks and amplifies its unique spot on the globe. Like a lens, it focuses and magnifies its particular time and location.

2. The essential medium of architecture is space and emptiness. Architecture is the construction of charged voids, frames of opportunity, and fields of possibility. I am interested in space more than meaning, an architecture of movement, of time, and of event rather than object and monument. I am interested in the emptiness that material constructs and in the invisible. The generative ideas of modern architecture emerged from the consideration of buildings as systems related to machines, natural organisms, or the phenomena of the city.

3. I search for the highest common denominator in order to establish the field of operation as a framework of unity and a panorama of resistance. I am interested in the art of mathematics that deals with the logic of quantity, shape, and arrangement; which entails the study of patterns providing unifying generalizations for fields and subfields; and in the science of structure, which enables one to focus on the encompassing and the comprehensive, the inclusive and the universal.

4. The building should be seen as an apparatus rather than an object, as an instrument rather than monument. I think of architecture as a support for dynamic human events rather than favoring programmatic norms and stasis. I have always resisted the idea of programming as authoritarian and aim instead for the generic and the general.

5. The final purpose is to provide an opportunity for the unique and the specific to be ultimately determined through the process of occupation. I tend to emphasize the authentic rather than the image. To this end, materials and systems of assembly and the processes of construction become the mutually aesthetic. I want to make objects that reveal their primary cause and create buildings that are predicated on perceptual processes. I like to think of construction as growth, not as idealized form, but as the actual performing of the work made precious. I think less about architecture as visual art than architecture as cooking. I make buildings by the gathering and assembling of ingredients; the plan is the recipe.

6. Traditionally the tools of architecture favor the static. Against which we need to focus on the way that buildings, by contrast, live in the river of time. Light and shadow reveal the passage of time, by virtue of their changing presence from day to night. They are thus able to frame works for gathering and seasonal celebration and thereby to express the processes of occupancy.

7. The value of sustainability causes us to focus on intelligent solutions, working with nature, using solar orientation, shading, day-lighting, window layering, energy harvesting from solar and wind technologies, or cooling from geothermal wells. We use wholesome materials and renewable resources and build lightly, using the least possible material and effort to encompass the optimum in terms of volume and space. Simplicity and synthesis are our goals. Simplicity is the property of being clear and concise, the principle of economy and succinctness. Since the synthesis is the property of complex elements being organized into hierarchies and groups, elements are condensed without reducing functionality. Our entire practice revolves around ideas of economy and optimization.

Brigitte Shim and Howard Sutcliffe

Brigitte Shim and Howard Sutcliffe formed the design practice Shim-Sutcliffe Architects in 1994, reflecting their shared interest and passion for the integration of architecture, landscape, and furniture. Their built architectural work has been honored with eleven Royal Architectural Institute of Canada Governor General's Medals and Awards for Architecture. Irrespective of scale, their work is engaged in densifying urban centers and in rethinking ways to build in the Canadian landscape

Brigitte Shim was born in Kingston, Jamaica in 1958, and was educated at the University of Waterloo, receiving degrees in Environmental Studies and Architecture. She worked successively for Arthur Erickson in Vancouver and for Baird Sampson Neuert Architects in Toronto. As a member of the architecture, landscape, and design faculty in the University of Toronto, she has taught a broad range of architectural design studios and lecture courses in the history and theory of landscape architecture. She has been a visiting professor at Yale University, the Ecole Polytechnique Federale de Lausanne, and Harvard University. In 2007 she served on the Aga Khan Architecture Award Master Jury.

Howard Sutcliffe was born in Yorkshire, England in 1958 and was educated at the University of Waterloo, where he received degrees in Environmental Studies and Architecture. After graduating he would work successively for Paul Merrick of Vancouver and for Ronald Thom, Barton Myers, and Kuwabara Payne McKenna Blumberg Architects of Toronto. In 1991, Sutcliffe was the first recipient of the Ronald J. Thom Award for early design achievement from the Canada Council.

Brigitte Shim and Howard Sutcliffe
The Craft of Place

Kenneth Frampton is passionate about architecture and has been sharing his enthusiasm, optimism, and infectious love of the discipline for a long time. It is fitting to honor Frampton on his 80th birthday, in an auditorium where he has spent decades sharing his ideas and his insights into projects and built work with generations of architecture students. These activities are an extension of who Kenneth Frampton is and reflects what he has been doing so brilliantly for many years.

One of the things you should know about Shim-Sutcliffe is that to date, we have built a relatively small body of work but we have been focused and committed to the realization of our ideas about architecture into built form. We have been practicing for about sixteen years and our studio has eight architects, including Howard and me. Our projects straddle public and private commissions, including public parks, sacred spaces, small institutions, and residential projects. Most of our built work is located near Toronto, Canada, where we live and work. Knowing a place through its geomorphology, climate, and cultural history allows us to more accurately balance between the wild and unpredictable forces of nature and the controlled processes of contemporary fabrication. Our work is situated between these two extreme conditions.

We are very fortunate to work with exemplary clients who have provided us with the opportunity to experiment at both small and large scales. For us, the exploration of conceptual ideas through the physical medium of architecture is the foundation of our practice. The enduring question of light and its role in northern latitude is a preoccupation of ours. We completed a house in a back alley in Toronto, the Laneway House (1993), centering around a light-filled interior courtyard lined with an exterior concrete finish that transformed the space into an exterior court.

In Canada, we occupy an enormous landmass with a tiny population. Whether one lives in the countryside or in the city, the mythological Canadian landscape permeates our lives. A recent project, the Ravine Guest House (2004), creates a covered outdoor space that provides a modern foreground to framed views of the indigenous forest of black locust, walnuts, and beeches.

Winter is a very long season in Canada. We imagine our work on a verdant summer day, and we also imagine our work in the middle of a winter snowstorm. We think about our buildings from both outside in and from inside out. We have always been preoccupied with this push and pull between inside and outside and the deliberate blurring of these physical boundaries in a northern latitude.

The majority of our work is located at the bottom edge of the Canadian Shield, described as a stone necklace of ancient metamorphic rock wrapping around Hudson's Bay. The Group of Seven—Canadian artists active during the 1920s and '30s—were among the first to depict the Canadian landscape not as pristine and pastoral, but as a raw and rugged wilderness. These artists found beauty in the untamed landscape, and have shaped our current perception of our land and our landscape.

Each of the following three projects—The Harrison Island Camp (2010), Congregation Bet Ha'am (2008), and The Integral House (2009)—was preceded by an earlier experiment that directly informed our design thinking. The Harrison Island Camp (2010) owes much of its invention to The Moorelands Camp Dining Hall (2002). The changing light conditions in the sacred space for the Congregation Bet Ha'am (2008) are preceded by the light experiments embedded in the one-room Craven Road Studio (2006). The Island House (2001) and its sectional exploration revealing the landscape directly inspired The Integral House (2008).

Moorelands Camp Dining Hall
Lake Kawagama, Haliburton, Ontario, Canada, 2002

This summer camp is located in Haliburton, about a two-hour drive north of Toronto, on the Canadian Shield. The building was designed for a nonprofit charity, Moorelands Community Services, dedicated to helping inner city children and youth in poverty since 1917. The dining hall is an inexpensive seasonal camp building. We combined an inexpensive industrial greenhouse glazing system with glulam structural frames, steel rods, and natural cedar to create a luminous gathering space for the camp community. From the arrival dock, the articulation and separation of all the building's walls and roof elements are visible. The main space is defined by 2" × 4" wood elements located below a readymade skylight inserted along the center ridge in the main space. This central zenithal light monitor is built up out of a series of additive repetitive wooden elements transforming the space into a register of light and a monitor of time. The overall structure is a mixture of structural glulam wood, frame construction, and invented steel trusses. We have a penchant for hybrid structures that drives our structural engineer crazy because wood and steel have different rates of expansion and contraction.

Moorelands Camp Dining Hall, 2002. Aerial view including Lake Kawagama

Entry dock facade

While we were in the early stages of design, we observed the camp staff close-up their buildings at the end of the summer season by fastening large pieces of plywood into the soft wood window frames. We responded by designing a series of integrated brise-soleils that provide shading for the dining hall during the hottest parts of a summer day and are also used to close the building for the winter season. These same brise-soleil elements also create intimate outdoor spaces during the summer, designed at the scale of the campers.

The final bay of the dining hall is covered but open, forming an outdoor porch—a recurring vernacular element. The new building capitalizes on its understanding of these very local conditions and uses this knowledge to reassemble and reconsider these elements in new ways.

Moorelands Camp Dining Hall. Detail view showing shutters over the deck in elevated position

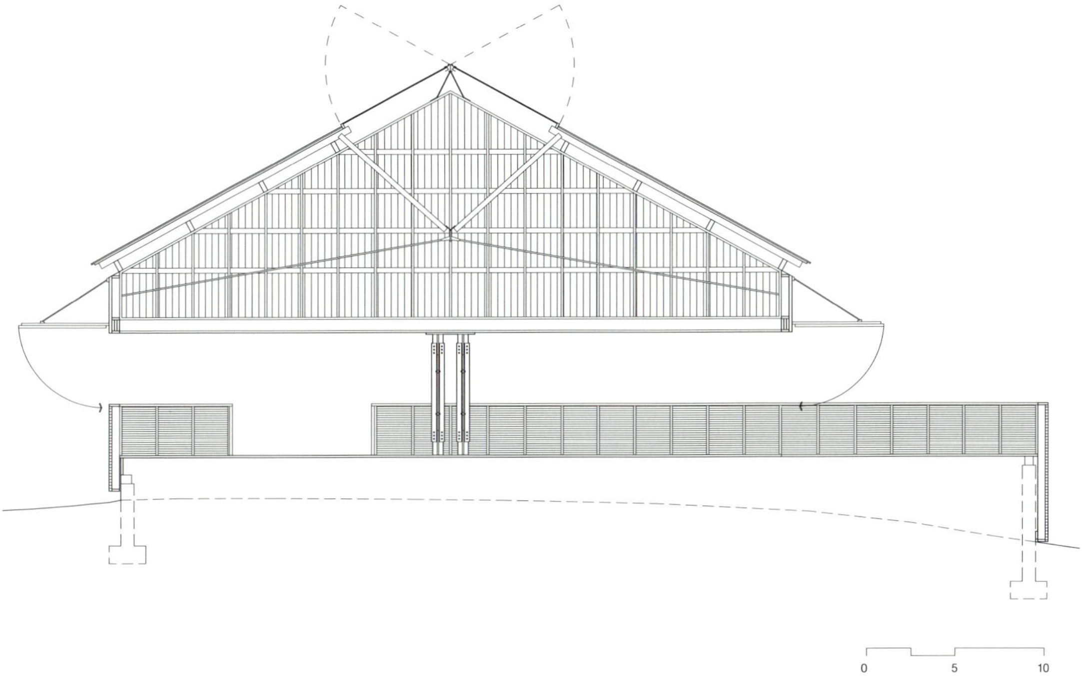

Section showing operative flaps and shutters

Corresponding interior view

Harrison Island Camp
Georgian Bay, Ontario, Canada, 2010

While we were designing the Harrison Island Camp, we were able to absorb and synthesize many of the lessons we learned from the Moorelands Camp Dining Hall project. We were inspired by the work of Canadian artist Paterson Ewen (1925–2002), who was often referred to as the "router guy," because he worked with plywood instead of canvas and would use a router to gouge out powerful images of earthbound and celestial phenomena. We designed an artist's studio for Paterson where he worked until he passed away. The way Ewen's work interpreted natural phenomena, such as the movement of stars, the falling of rain, patterns of lightning, the movement of clouds, and charting of turbulent weather, reminds us of the power embedded in natural forces.

We imagined the Harrison Island Camp as a wooden tent. Our early sketches explore the possibility of the main space becoming an outdoor porch set into a rugged landscape. The building's foundations are set on a grid of scaffolding screw jack bases, which was our way of ensuring that we would touch the ancient post-glacial rock as lightly as possible. We developed this project by building a series of conceptual and physical models, which enabled us to develop the structural system and shape the space simultaneously.

The site for this project is a granite island, which is part of an archipelago of Thirty Thousand Islands in Georgian Bay of Lake Huron. We developed the building idea and then imagined how one would realize it in a remote location. Every component had to travel by road and barge and then be carried by two people over a rocky terrain to the building site. Lightness and maneuverability of building materials were important design considerations. We built a full-size mock-up of a structural bay and asked our structural engineers to verify its stability. The physical mock-up enabled us to make each component as light as possible. We transported all the Structural Insulated Panels (SIPs) for the floors, walls, and roof from the marina by barge and then onto the island where each panel was carried by hand to the building site.

The light monitor developed for the Moorelands Camp Dining Hall project responded to the client's program, the need for natural ventilation and lots of light along with the structural imperative to create a large column free space. The Harrison Island Camp absorbs the lessons of the earlier experiments while rethinking and reconsidering the role of light and structure in this new porch space. The shaped wood ceiling and metal trusses were fabricated in controlled conditions over the winter months. The building is designed to be assembled, disassembled, transported, and reassembled on a remote island location. The challenge of building in nonurban locations required that we recalibrate our approach to craftsmanship and fabrication.

The Harrison Island Camp contrasts a horizontally framed view of dense forest with an expansive panoramic view from the porch looking out over the water and the Canadian Shield landscape. A series of sliding fiberglass panels allows the user to continually adjust and modify the degree of enclosure and view, depending on the orientation of the prevailing wind and the angle of the sun.

Harrison Island Camp, 2010. View of the barge delivering the prefabricated components to the site

Harrison Island Camp, Georgian Bay, ON, 2010. Completed cabin

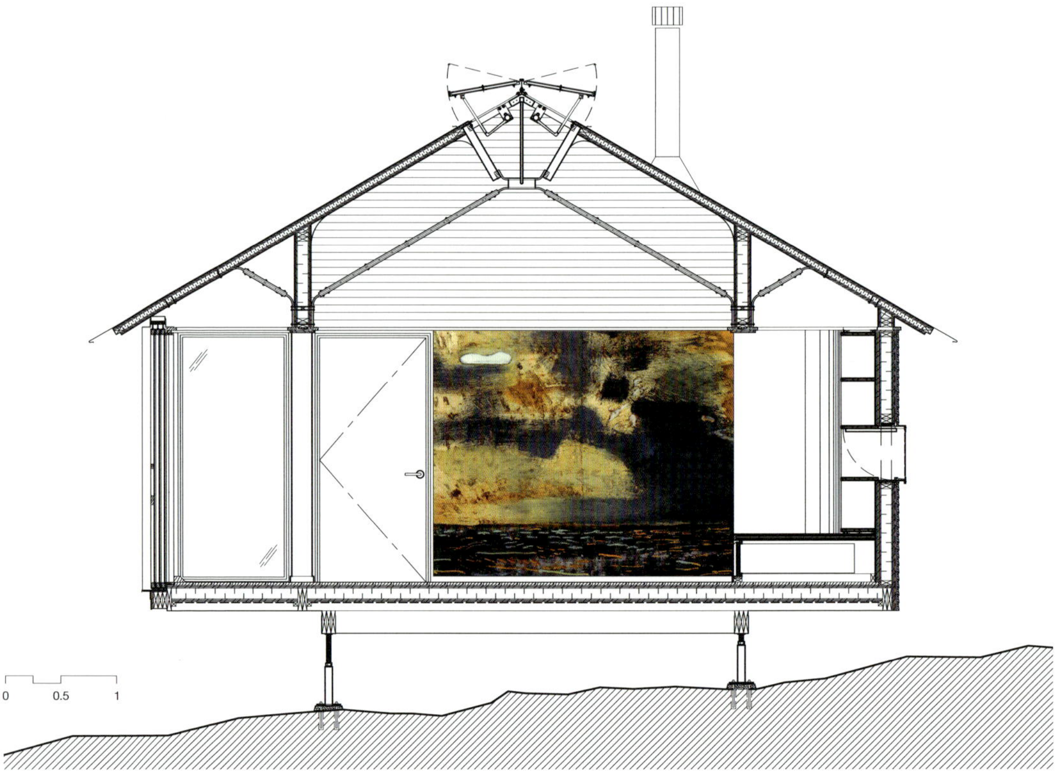

Harrison Island Camp. Interior view

Cross section showing the screw jack supports and light-weight trussed structure and roof vents

Craven Road Studio
Toronto, Ontario, Canada, 2006

The Craven Road Studio is located in the urban core of Toronto. We designed a red, plywood-clad house in a back alley in Toronto in 1996, for an architect and archivist. A decade later, the same client asked us to design a new studio adjacent to his existing house. This project is a single room that explores the amplification and articulation of natural light. Our client, Robert Hill, has an extensive working architectural reference library, including a large collection of architectural posters, books, magazines, and photographs. He asked us to provide him with a light-filled space with no glare and a place to view and display art. A narrow skylight lines the perimeter of the building, illuminating all four walls with natural light. The articulated sectional detail sets off the floating ceiling and disguises the fact that walls are often housing deep storage cabinets.

Natural light washes the upper wood fins, providing even light for the white display walls below. The amplified light illuminates this single room throughout the day, creating a sanctuary both inside and out.

Craven Road Studio, Toronto, ON, 2006. Exterior view at night

Interior looking out toward the courtyard

Bet Ha'am Synagogue
Portland, Maine, 2007

The Craven Road Studio explores the passage of light in a single room tracking, its transformation through the day and through the seasons. This experiment directly informed the design of the Bet Ha'am Synagogue in Portland, Maine. In this project, light became an essential building element, directly linked to our spatial exploration. Depending on the time of the day, the time of the year, and the angle of the sun, one registers the light in front of the wooden baffle or behind it. Natural light bathes the wooden clapboard walls, creating thin horizontal shadows that transform rapidly from day to night, continually registering exterior as well as interior shifts.

The section through the building is asymmetrical with the deeper west side capturing and embracing the sunset while the east side holds the morning light. The changing quality of the light registers the movement of the sun throughout the day transforming hour by hour ensuring that one is constantly aware of one's relationship to nature.

Bet Ha'am Synagogue, Portland, ME, 2007. West wall of sanctuary with afternoon light washing canted wall and light baffle.

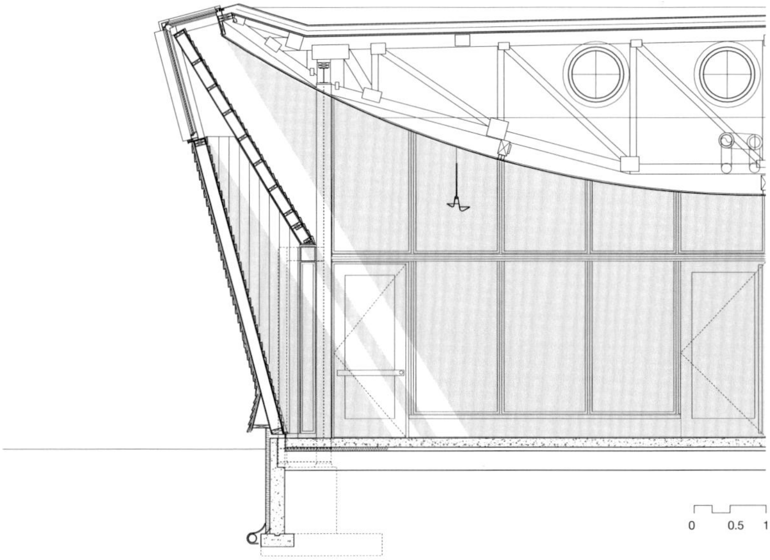

Island House
Howe Island, St. Lawrence River, Ontario, Canada, 2001

Island House (2001) would eventually become the point of departure for The Integral House (2009). It was designed for a five-acre site on an island, which is one of the Thousand Islands in the St. Lawrence River, between New York State and Southern Ontario. This house is located on Howe Island, which has been devoted to dairy farming for generations. Today this pastoral landscape is being transformed into suburbia. Our first action on the site was to build a retaining wall parallel to the country road and the river shoreline, extending from inside to outside and forming the backbone of the site. Our second action was to hydro-seed the entire property with a local clover mixture. The clover smells amazing in the springtime and reinforces the longstanding agricultural use. A local farmer harvests the clover meadow several times a year, retaining the agricultural cycles that are a key part of the local culture.

From the entry, one looks into the upper portion of the main living space where the landscape view is obscured by a fiberglass screen wall. One descends down a few feet via stairs to the main space, which is a cubic volume surrounded by water on three sides. The panoramic views of the landscape that are not visible upon entry are revealed after descending into the main space. The lush water garden serves as a thematic link to the St. Lawrence River, and reinforces the island metaphor. The corners of the main living space are defined by large sliding doors that open up, transforming the space into a three-dimensional screened-in porch.

Water becomes a predominant element, registering light and landscape making the ephemeral visible. In this project, the water landscape is as powerful as the ground landscape; one penetrating into the other and vice versa.

Detailed section through the synagogue showing arrangment of light baffles

Island House, Howe Island, St. Lawrence River, Ontario, 2001. View of water garden

Interior of living room

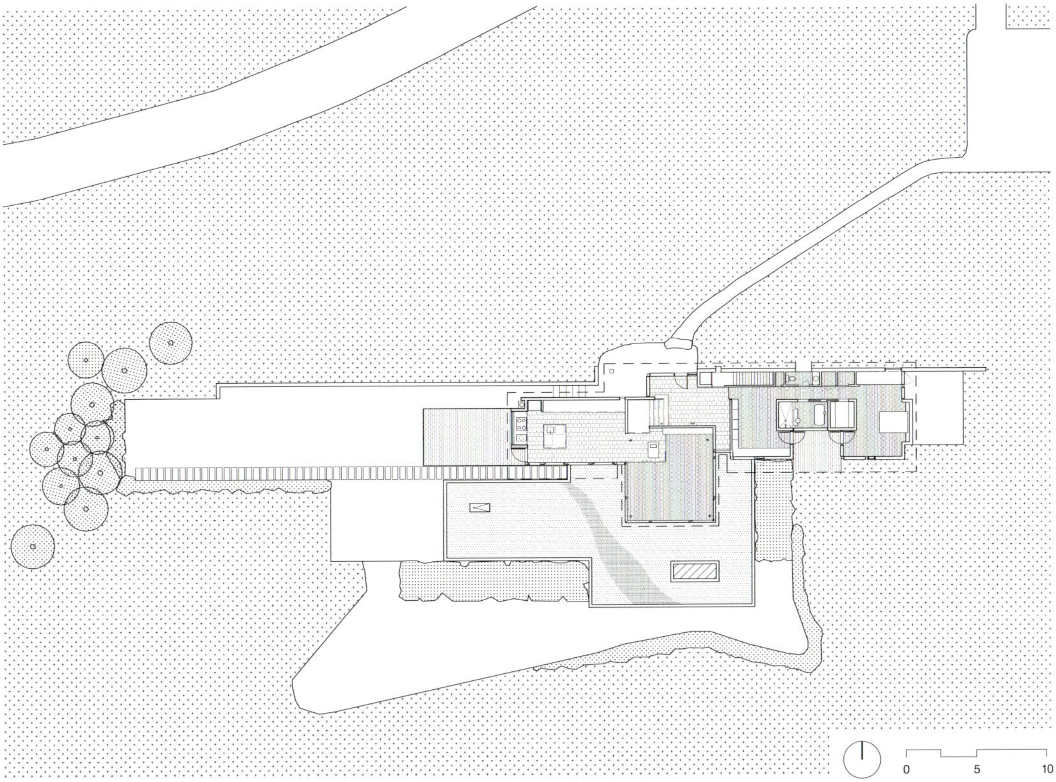

Site plan showing different surface treatments inside and out

Interior of living room looking out over the lily pond

Island House. View of the house with clover meadow in the foreground

The Integral House
Toronto, Ontario, Canada, 2009

The journey through the Island House and its obscuring and subsequent revealing of the landscape is explored and investigated further in the design of The Integral House. This project was commissioned by a gifted mathematician, who is also a concert violinist. It sounds like an exercise that might be assigned as a first-year studio in an architecture school. The mathematician-musician asked for curves, reflecting his passion for calculus, lots of glass, an integrated art installation, and the creation of a performance space for 150 friends in a residential living room on a steep sloping site. You can tell from our earlier projects that we had not used a lot of curves prior to designing The Integral House. It took us a while to digest, synthesize, and rethink curvilinear forms in our work. We built a lot of physical three-dimensional models, in order to think about the building's interior and the potential of providing fluid, uninterrupted spaces.

The Integral House section is a key element linking the lessons learned from the Island House but translated to a steeper slope and more complex building program. The building section is only a portion of a more dramatic site section beginning with a residential neighborhood at the top and extending down a steep ravine slope to the main performance space and then descending farther to the river valley. The journey from street to the main performance space allows one to enter and occupy the ravine landscape without ever going outside.

The main performance space has an undulating inner wooden perimeter, creating a newly inscribed contour line shaping and forming the main space. Shaped wooden fins of varied depths and different orientations are used to define the space by obscuring the landscape while also providing sun shading.

In this project, we experimented with many aspects of computer fabrication. We moved back and forth between our design sketches and physical cardboard models, clay models, and three-dimensional computer printouts to aid us in

The Integral House, 2009. View along the flat bottom of the Don River valley in the foreground with downtown Toronto beyond

the development of fittings such as door handles, balustrades, handrails, and custom bronze clips.

We designed processes to ensure a high level of craftsmanship in the project. Every fabricator bidding on the wooden interior fin package had to produce a full size vertical fin with the submission. This full-size mock-up allowed us to fully understand each fabricator's definition of workmanship and his specific approach to fabricating a vertical wooden fin. It was instructive observing such varied approaches to building the same element resulting from the same construction drawings. Much of North American construction wraps a building in many layers, similar to layers of outdoor adventure clothing, with thinner and thicker layers, for different conditions. At The Integral House, one does not actually read a window frame because the double-glazed units gets slotted into the sides of shaped wooden fins extending out and protruding into the interior. The shaped wooden fins create an abstract forest foreground in the main volume, thereby registering the subtle shifts of light and ephemeral atmospheric conditions.

Architects today have the ability to use computer fabrication to do things that a decade ago would be very expensive, labor intensive, and difficult to realize. We produced laser-cut metal templates fabricated from our digital drawings and used these as a datum and reference points for the undulating curving walls during the on-site construction. We are fascinated by and interested in the crucial role that interim construction elements play in realizing complex forms.

The Integral House, Toronto, ON, 2009. Study model of the building situated on a steep slope overlooking the river valley

1 Fountain
2 Pool
3 Terrace
4 Exercise Room
5 Water Closet
6 Change Room
7 Shower/Steam Room
8 Sauna
9 Mechanical Room
10 Elevator

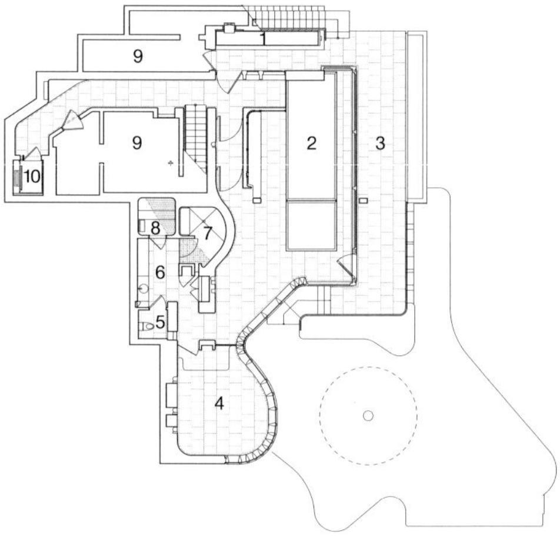

1 Entry
2 Reflecting Pool
3 Upper Living Room
4 Dining Room
5 Kitchen
6 Pantry
7 Garage
8 Elevator

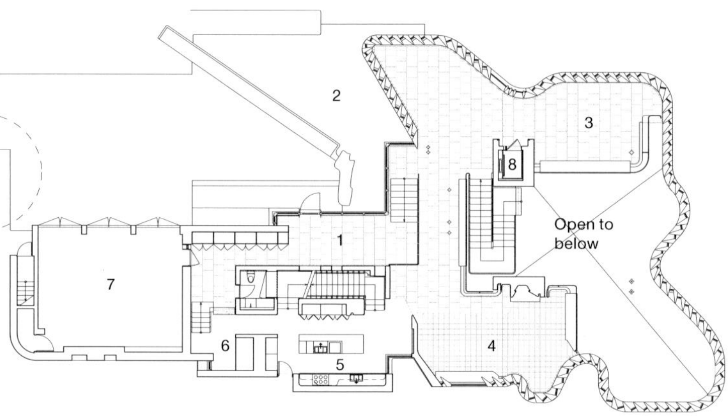

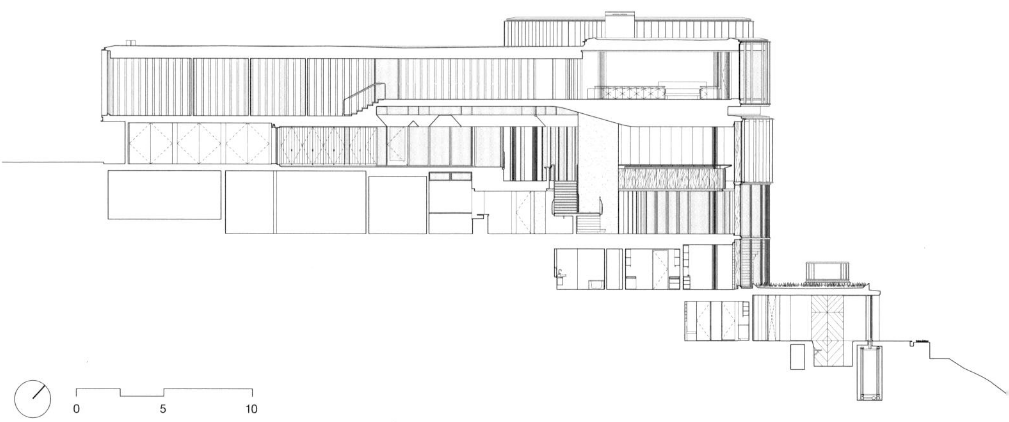

The Integral House. Top to bottom: lower ground floor plan, entry floor, and cross section

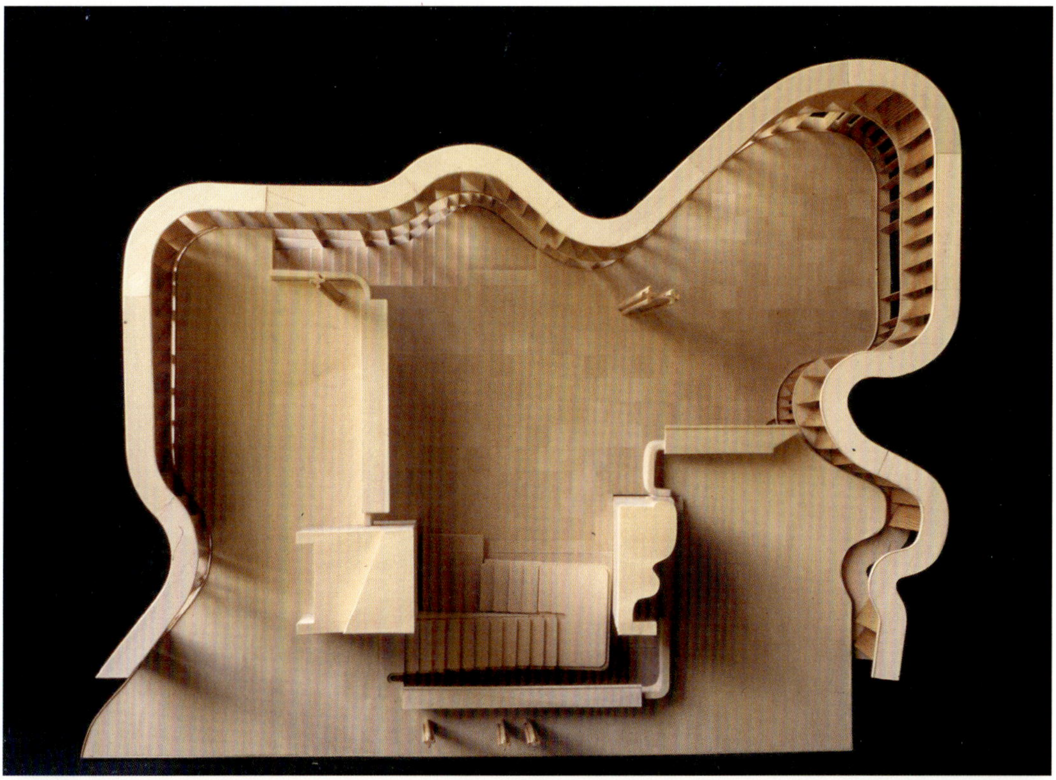

Plan view of wooden study model

View of living room from the entry level

The Integral House. Interior of main living room and performance space during summer

Toronto's ravine system has been described as "San Francisco turned upside down," referring to its hidden topography. The ravine system is a dynamic ecology situated in the heart of a dense urban metropolis. The Integral House reinterprets the ravine's contours and captures its particular light quality by rearticulating its steep slope, providing a fitting foreground to this found natural feature. The building's undulating curved facade is evident from the ravine elevation and transforms as it moves toward the neighborhood. Shaped etched-glass panels with convex and concave curves hover above an oak wall, defining The Integral House from the street. The outer curvilinear etched-glass skin sandwiches an air space containing LED lights and a double-glazed sealed unit on the other side. These elements are combined to create a new wall assembly that is luminous during the day and transforms into a liquid illuminated glass surface at night. The Integral House entry directs your view downward to the main performance space. Sensual curvilinear railings and balustrades guide you to the lower level of the double-height performance space. The descent downward to the main space allows one to view the landscape through a wooden curtain, opening up to reveal Toronto's majestic ravine system. This project blurs the line between the natural and the constructed, and nature and building. Understanding the subtle transformation of light from day to night and from summer to winter in The Integral House recalibrates our understanding of the four seasons.

We collaborated with glass artist Mimi Gellman and our structural engineer David Bowick to create a blue glass stair installation. In this private stair, laminated, hand-blown blue glass shingles are supported by bronze clips held in place by taut stainless steel cables. The blue glass stair can be read as a large stringed instrument viewed from different parts of the house, foreshadowing the space beyond. A skylight over the blue glass stair along with glass treads allow natural light to filter through the stair to the lower level. Many different performances, from contemporary dance to chamber music groups, have been held at The Integral House. Many musicians have described the experience of performing at The Integral House as playing within or "performing in an instrument." We were interested in creating fluidity between inside and outside, between public and private, between performance space and ravine space.

For Howard and I, architecture fuses together poetic ideas, inert materials, physical site, and specific social conditions. Architecture trades on its ability to touch and shape people's lives in profound and meaningful ways. We hope that these projects afford you an insight into our iterative design process and the crucial role that light, water, and landscape play in our work.

The Integral House. Entry level

Stairs leading down to the recital volume

Rick Joy

Rick Joy was born in 1958 in Dover-Foxcroft, Maine, has over 21 years of experience as an architect and builder, and is the founding principal of Rick Joy Architects. His architectural career began with a three-year appointment on the design team of Phoenix Central Library, working under the direction of the architect William Bruder. Since opening his own office in 1992, Joy has designed and built numerous private and commercial commissions and was the Partner of I-10 Studio, an architecture and planning firm he established solely for the design and realization of the Amangiri Resort in Utah.

In 2002, he received the American Academy of Arts and Letters Award in Architecture, and in 2004 won the prestigious National Design Award from the Smithsonian Institution, Cooper-Hewitt National Design Museum. He has served as a visiting professor at Harvard University's Graduate School of Design, Rice University, and Massachusetts Institute of Technology. He is currently an adjunct professor of architecture at the University of Arizona.

Rick Joy
Proximity and Distance

I am enormously grateful and honored by Kenneth's warm and personal invitation to participate in this conference in honor of his 80th birthday.

As an architect I am based in Tucson, Arizona for myriad reasons that are important to me. Most significantly, the richness and the diversity of the different cultures that coexist there, the extraordinary beauty of the Sonoran Desert and the greater American Southwest are reasons that continue to keep me there. However, I am originally from Maine. I lived there until I was 28 and part of my nature comes from being a Mainer. Living in and around the very simple and deliberately crafted coastal structures has had a significant influence on my work as an architect.

The culture of Maine life has had a similar impact. For example, in Maine we generally communicate via very shortly constructed and deliberate conversational crispness. No extra words. In fact, these days, when we meet one another on the street we say, "Good, and you?" because it is a waste of time to first ask, "Hey, how are you?" It is much the same with building. If one were to install an ornamental detail on his house, the entire town would notice and comment. It has changed a little now. I can also say that my interest in the atmospheric qualities of experiences began in Maine as a child. I recall being very much drawn to the fog and the woodsy experience there. I would row my boat out into the middle of the fog and just hang out there. My friends would wonder about my sanity, but it meant something to me that I did not understand at the time.

After being a road musician and carpenter for 11 years, I moved to Tucson to study architecture at the University of Arizona. I was motivated to obtain a degree from a quality state school, get registered, and start making buildings as quickly as possible. There I discovered the American West and specifically the fantastic Sonoran Desert. The desert is at times a dream-like fantasy of a landscape that teaches one to slow down and observe the small things. It is within this personal search and the hope of understanding small things that the more ethereal sensory ground inspires me and comes though in my work.

Since moving to Arizona, I have spent a great deal of time in the raw wilds of the Sonoran Desert. The most significant experiences have been in the slot canyons. They are nearly inaccessible places, where the scale, the smells, the tactile qualities, in particular, the light qualities are moving. There is a lovely, nuanced world in and around Tucson that continues to entice me and my colleagues to understand the elusive elements of truth in that otherwise mystified setting.

This sensitivity to place has made me more aware of the possibilities of value-added experiential nuances we can offer our clients. Generous sidelights, such as are used in the main sitting area of the Convent Studios, allow a person sitting there to be bathed in golden sunlight for optimal reading in a beautiful Vermeer-like scene as viewed from the kitchen. We found the best place on the site to position the cocktail terrace to help clients best experience the blue hour, done with the Tubac House. In another example, we helped the client of the Desert Nomad House live in the shadows of the Tucson Mountains with a very discreet, up-close, and personal relationship with the landscape and yet remain slightly removed from it.

The works of art that touch me most are works that somehow induce precise considerations or reflections about a place, ourselves, or natural phenomena. I am enormously influenced by the minimalist landscape artists of the American West, such as James Turrell, the installation artist who offers self-awareness and new perception of the subtle changes in our surroundings; or Donald Judd, who worked with deliberate shapes and positions in a landscape; or Olafur Eliasson, the Icelandic artist who taunts the viewer's awareness, via natural phenomena, claiming that he is actually perceiving more specifically at a specific point in time. His work had a strong influence on the long entry hallway at our Taos Hacienda. The earthen barrel-vaulted hall is built with no electric light of its own. The space is simply the receiver of the light and ambience of each of the adjacent spaces, with a wide range of color temperatures spilling from each room. One can find other influences and parallels in my architecture.

Similarly, I consider the buildings we make to be instruments that frame views and experiences, helping the inhabitants to have an experience of nature and place in their daily lives—essentially, staging lifestyles. Juhani Pallasmaa says it best when he says that the act of looking through the window is more important than a window itself, that it is more about the verb than the noun. We can make great windows but, the act of looking through a window or stepping through a threshold is the first thought. The Catalina House was my first house and in many ways I believe it is my most soulful work to date. It is the rabbit in my chase to achieve as good a house again. I will compare two early projects in detail, which demonstrate the depth of concept and detail that is important to me.

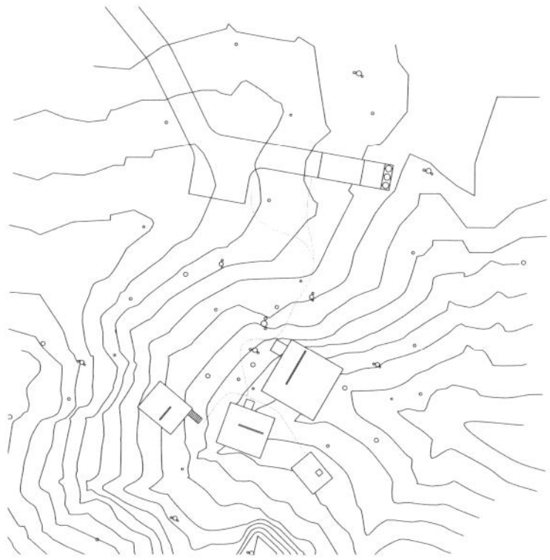

Desert Nomad House
Tucson, Arizona, 2005

This is a house where the experience of nature and light is the principal consideration. Three primary program spaces define a specific prospect for each. The house is split into three detached, independent volumes. The combined kitchen, living, and dining room has a beautiful view of the Catalina Mountains. When the sun is setting, the mountain range behind makes everything in the foreground dark and so the distant mountains become a bright, well-lit, and beautiful sculpture with changing colors as the reverse-sunset closes the day and the city lights come up. The bedroom has a beautiful view of a ridge where the sun comes up and hits the tip of the ridge, resulting in a bright spot. As the sun rises, the light descends on this hill and backlights all the ocotillo and saguaro needles in the more immediate landscape. There is also a little framed still life of the close-up desert seen from the window of the den.

The large box is the combined kitchen, living, and dining room; the medium box is the bedroom; and the small one is the little den. These three boxes are elevated so that the flora, fauna, and water can flow underneath them. They are also elevated so as to provide a single aperture in each space, which serves as both a light source and a viewing aperture. In realizing the building, we decided to emphasize the applied skin nature of the box. Thus the exterior was clad in heavy steel plate with a very precise patterning, while the interior was finished with maple, using the same pattern. The roof deck is made of teak and there is a cavity below the deck to shade the roof. The net result gives the effect of slicing into a steel box so as to reveal the wood core within. However, the real art of this house is the owner, who lives there beautifully.

Desert Nomad House, Tucson, AZ, 2005. Ground floor plan and site plan

Desert Nomad House. View of the three self-contained prisms

Night view of the interior

Distant views of the complex at night

Living room interior

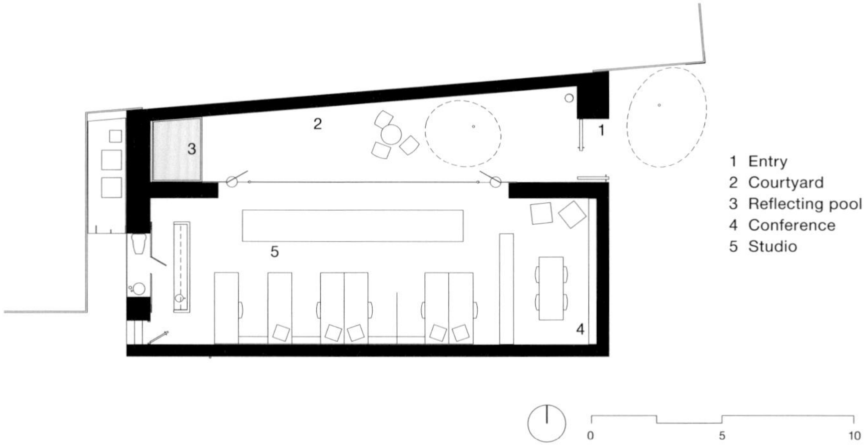

Rubio Avenue Studio
Tucson, Arizona, 1999

In contrast to the Desert Nomad House, the Rubio Avenue Studio, where my offices are located, is a building of walls. I decided to enclose it with walls because I am easily distracted and I wanted to create an introspective space. I believe that the most beautiful wall is one that starts from the ground and reaches the sky uninterrupted. Here the 14-foot (4.3 m) high walls are made of compacted earth.

In the studio there is a north-facing window wall between the inside and the outside courtyard. To make this window wall I tried to do the same thing, that is, to bring a glass wall up from the ground and allow it reach the sky uninterrupted. The south sun hits the north wall of the courtyard and provides enough natural daylight for us throughout the day. On the inside the reflective silver ceiling is a play on the "blue ceiling" outside—the blue sky that we experience 360 days a year in Tucson.

I thought when I started my practice that five desks would be plenty, but after only a few years we replaced them with one big table in the middle for 12 people. It is a fun office with an international presence. Currently Austria, Germany, Portugal, Korea, Vietnam, Greece, Mexico, Croatia, and China are represented here.

Rubio Avenue Studio, Tucson, AZ, 1999. Plan

Rubio Avenue Studio with adjacent patio

View of the studio interior

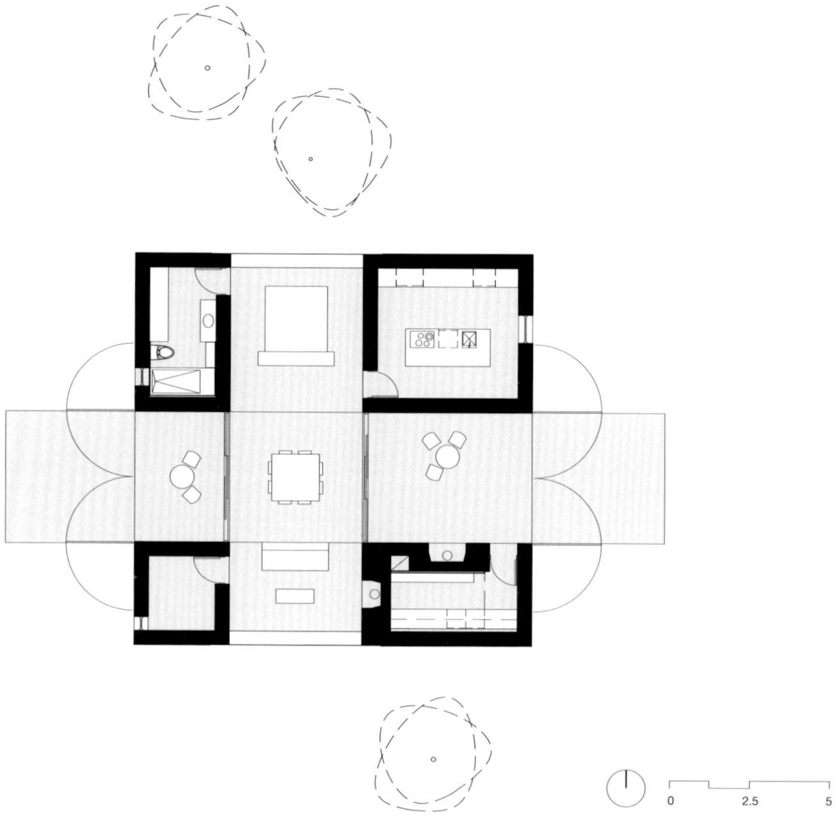

Adobe Canyon House
Patagonia, Arizona, 2005

At first glance, the house appears as a single massive block of rammed earth on a hill. Evocative of an ancient ruin, the block is 42-foot (12.8 m) square with 14-foot-high (4.3 m) walls. This mass-form encloses an asymmetrically placed cruciform volume accommodating the social functions of living and dining. To the south and north of this centroid are the lounge and bedroom respectively, while the other quadrants enclosed by thick, compacted earth walls are, on the north side, the bathroom and kitchen, and on the south, the Bikram Yoga room and a store. In contrast to the blank external surface, there are four large openings, one on each side of the mass; two of them, on the north and south, are filled with glass while the eastern and western openings take the form of recessed covered terraces that are linked by full-height sliding glass walls to the ventral living/dining volume. These terraces, receiving sunrise and sunset, respectively, may be closed off when necessary by full-height stainless steel doors. The large glazed openings on the northern and southern faces are protected by activated shade screens.

Adobe Canyon House, Patagonia, AZ, 2005. Plan

General view of house and site

Close-up view of the house at twilight

Amangiri Resort
Canyon Point, Utah, 2009

The recently completed resort and spa in Utah was an 11-year collaboration with two partners: Marwan Al-Sayed and Wendell Burnette. We formed a firm called I-10 Studio, named for the interstate highway on which we spent so much time commuting while working on this project.

The site is in a landscape reminiscent of old Marlboro Man advertisements, with immense space, towering mesas, sheer walls, and a giant blue sky. The real allure of the land is quietly hidden in its wildness. The land moves one to recall all that is pure and wild about the American West. With our 21st-century eyes we can see the beauty, but only from a perspective largely isolated from the land—from either a car or in the movies. To truly feel the land one must experience it up close. That is the privileged experience of the resort.

The simple layout has 34 rooms strung along a 190-foot-high (57.9 m) rock formation like a pearl necklace, with the rooms flanking the main lobby and pool in the center. The emphasis is on water, rock, and sky. The buildings are designed as thick concrete masses, carved by program, movement, and light. The concrete has a very reflective quality and is the same color as the surrounding Entrada sandstone, intentionally rendered as abstract geology with colors that blend into the shifting landscape of sand, sage, and rock.

Individual rooms are entered through the thick concrete mass with dripping water bodies into a private screened court and from there, into a room that affords the guest an exclusive framed view to the landscape and mesas beyond. One idea that I have enjoyed the most is the idea that the bed and "campfire" are at the same level as the desert floor. Having spent much time in the desert, I appreciate the perspective of sitting low on the desert floor, which is far better than sitting up high on a chair. Visitors to the hotel are essentially sleeping at ground level like a very privileged cowboy.

Amangiri Resort, Canyon Point, UT, 2009. View of hotel swimming pool with the desert and the mountains in the background

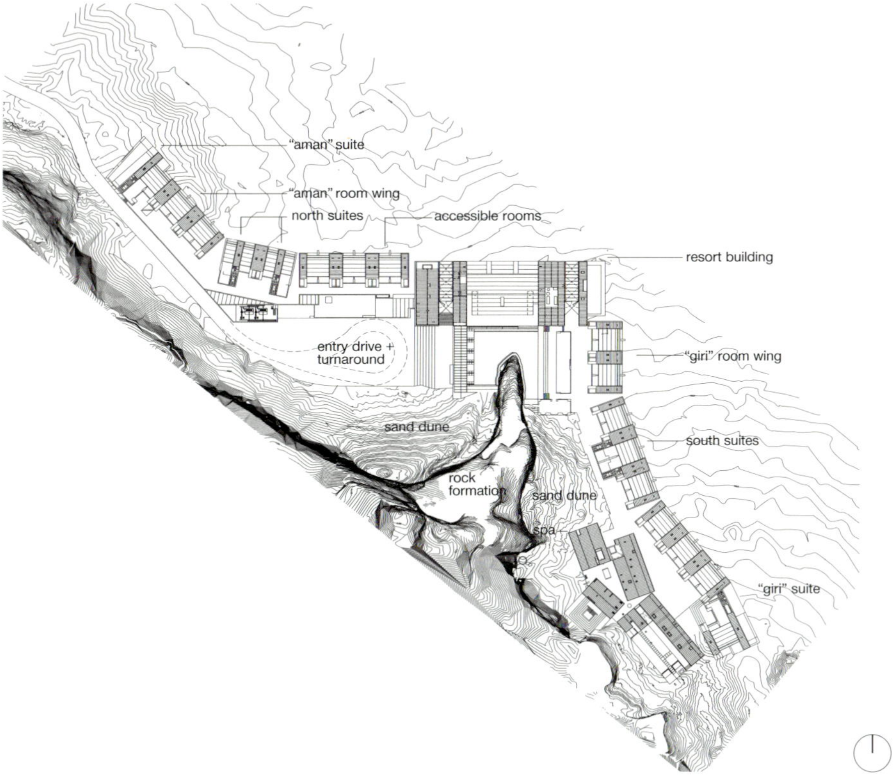

View of units against cliffs

Ground floor

Amangiri Resort. View of sun terrace

Detail of the hotel in relation to the surrounding landscape

Entry to hotel swimming pool

Woodstock Farm
Woodstock, Vermont, 2008

The house and barn are set at the base of a pastoral valley in the Green Mountains of Vermont. A clear stream runs from the top of the valley to a small pond created by an old stone dam. The heart of the house is centered around the pond. The main house is arranged in relation to the stone wall remnants from the previous farmhouse and is a simple elongated stone-ended gable with major view orientation to the fields and the pond to the north and large notched openings to the south that allow filtered light and shadows through the trees. Interior walls are clad with narrow spruce boards laid vertically.

The barn is fixed with a deliberate pond alignment and is designed as a more utilitarian two-story, multi-use gabled form with a guest bunkhouse upstairs and a garage and basketball court below. Each building is constructed of primary steel post and beam bents supporting a Structural Insulated Panel (SIP) system skin, which is clad on the exterior with flush detailed cedar shingles. House systems include geothermal heating and cooling and hydroelectric power. The Woodstock Farm project was thrilling because it was a homecoming of sorts for me.

In the end I hope you can feel our belief in honoring and drawing upon the building culture and spirit of place, whether it is compacted earth or weathered steel in the desert, Texas limestone for our Dallas and Marfa projects, cast concrete in California, Utah, and Chile, brick arches in Guadalajara, or even wood shingles in Vermont. This is a big part of the work. But it is the lifestyle propositions we offer to the clients that are the basis of our focus.

Woodstock Farm, Woodstock, VE, 2008. View of the complex in the landscape

1 Entry
2 Living
3 Kitchen
4 Pantry
5 Bedroom
6 Gallery
7 Master shower
8 Master bedroom
9 Master bathtub
10 Terrace
11 Loft hall
12 Guest suite
13 Bunk room
14 Studio/office
15 Basketball court below
16 Dock

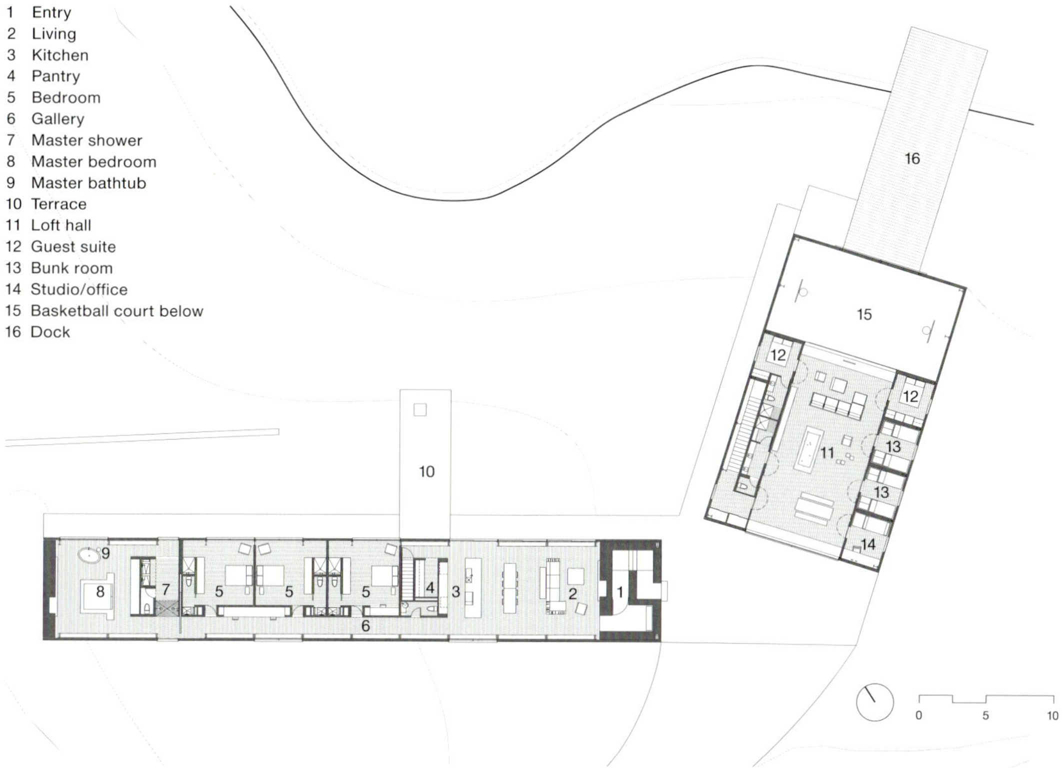

Ground floor plan

Exterior view of house showing sharp and tight eaves detailing

John and Patricia Patkau

John Patkau was born in Winnipeg, Manitoba in 1947 and graduated from the University of Manitoba with bachelor's degrees in Arts and in Environmental Studies in 1969, followed by a Master of Architecture, in 1972. He founded Patkau Architects in 1979 in Vancouver, British Columbia. The firm has received numerous awards including, thirteen Governor General's Medals, four Progressive Architecture Awards, sixteen Canadian Architect Awards of Excellence, an RAIC Innovation in Architecture Award of Excellence, three AIA Honor Awards, and the Royal Architectural Institute of Canada Gold Medal for lifetime achievement. John Patkau was created a member of the Order of Canada in recognition of his services to architecture and for his significant contribution to Canadian culture. Internationally, he is an Honorary Fellow of both the American Institute of Architects and the Royal Institute of British Architects. He has been a visiting professor at a number of universities, including Eero Saarinen Visiting Professor at Yale University, Eliot Noyes Professor of Architecture at Harvard University, and Raymond E. Moritz Distinguished Visiting Professor at Washington University. In 1997, he participated in the 7th International Alvar Aalto Symposium in Jyväskylä, Finland.

Patricia Patkau was born in Winnipeg, Manitoba in 1950 and graduated from the University of Manitoba with a Bachelor of Interior Design in 1973 and from Yale University with a Master of Architecture in 1978. Throughout her career she has been committed to both teaching and practice. She began her career as an academic at the University of California at Los Angeles where she taught from 1988 to 1990. In 1990 she returned to British Columbia and joined the faculty of the School of Architecture and Landscape Architecture at the University of British Columbia of which she is now an emeritus professor. Patricia is a Fellow of the Royal Architectural Institute of Canada, a member of the Royal Canadian Academy of Arts, an Honorary Fellow of the American Institute of Architects and the Royal Institute of British Architects, and a member of the Order of Canada. In March 2009, Patricia Patkau was awarded the Tau Sigma Delta Gold Medal for exemplary commitment to architectural education and to the practice of architecture.

John and Patricia Patkau
The Structure of Relationships

Kenneth Frampton's book, *Modern Architecture: A Critical History* (1980), and the essay "Towards a Critical Regionalism" (1983) coincided with the beginning of our practice. Together these texts had an enormous effect on us, helping us define who we are as architects. In many important ways, our work is a reflection of Kenneth's thinking. The Strawberry Vale School, the Grande Bibliothèque du Québec, and the Linear House reflect some of that thinking, as well as the diversity that exists within our practice. They reflect different scales and physical contexts, from the small, domestic, and rural to the large, public, and urban. Furthermore, they are situated in distinctly different climates and serve quite different communities.

Strawberry Vale School
Victoria, British Columbia, Canada, 1995

This is a public school for children from kindergarten to grade seven. It is located in Victoria on Vancouver Island on the Pacific coast. It sits within a suburban area on the edge of Victoria but, being adjacent to farm fields, retains something of a rural context.

The Strawberry Vale School was a breakthrough for us in that it arose from a fundamental change in our thinking about the relationship between the manmade and the natural. We had been in practice for about ten years when we designed this building, and up to this point we had thought of nature as landscape and as an aesthetic context complementing a building. With this project we began to think about nature as a system and about buildings as a part of that system. The design of the school is inspired by the environmental knowledge embedded in the vernacular language of rural buildings. Like such buildings, the structure aspires to give architectural form to natural forces.

The school is a replacement for another school that existed on the site, the foundations of which we retained as part of the play environment. We also relocated a single-room schoolhouse to serve as a gate house. We designed the entry sequence

beginning on the northern end of the site adjacent to the single-room schoolhouse, along a road that passes the foundations of the former elementary school, ultimately arriving at the new school, which is adjacent to a beautiful pocket park comprised of rock and Garry oak trees, a very distinctive species of oak that grows on Vancouver Island.

One side of the project is embedded in a "forest" of oak trees and the other side addresses a public entry sequence. Even though the northern side of the building has an informal geometry, it is still geometrical. It is intended to express the entry into a public building as something that receives people whereas the southern side embedded in the forest and rock is subordinate to the landscape.

The plan consists of sixteen classrooms organized into pods of four. All classrooms have direct access to the south while the northern side accommodates the gymnasium, a multi-purpose room, a library, and the administration as well as other supporting spaces. Meandering between these elements is the major circulation spine of the school. The irregular plan form is a direct response to the site. To minimize site disturbance, the location and elevation of each pod is adjusted to follow the contours of the land and avoid rock outcroppings. The irregular configuration of spine and pods creates a variety of non-programmed indoor and outdoor spaces that support educational and social interactions, both spontaneous and planned, thereby providing an architectural basis for a stronger sense of community within the school.

The section is elevated over the circulation spine because it is also the delivery system for the mechanical elements, which plays directly into some of the other strategies embedded in the school. Clerestory lighting is introduced in order to balance the luminosity within classroom interiors and create natural stack ventilation. Once the classrooms are ventilated, the air rises into the spine and is exhausted through displacements in section. The resulting exterior form is a direct expression of the sectional character of the building.

Strawberry Vale School, Victoria, BC, Canada, 1995

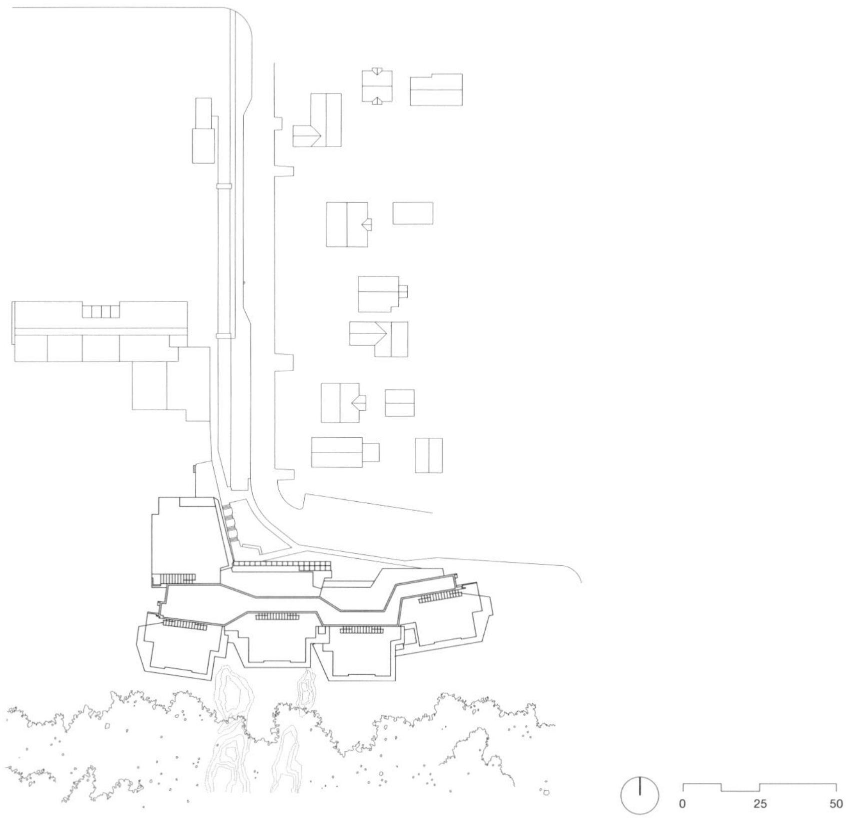

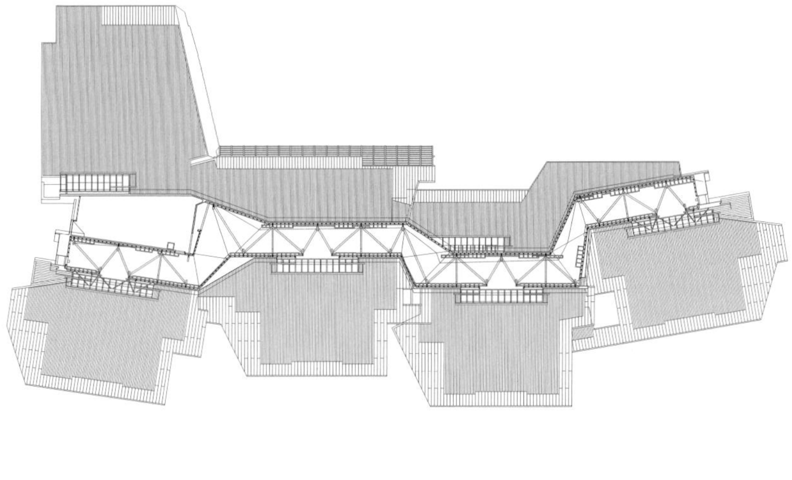

Site plan of the Strawberry Vale School in relation to the suburban context

Cutaway roof plan showing structural framework and servicing channel running along building spine

We wanted the building to respond to natural forces in terms of both its form and details. For example, the roof has two different claddings, corrugated over the main body of buildings with insulated spaces and flat-ribbed cladding over the uninsulated portions of the roof that extend beyond the interior of the school. The environmental performance of the roof is reflected directly in its form, as is the case with the walls and other components of the building.

On the south side overlooking the oak forest, the roof planes of the school rise fairly directly from the ground plane. In between the pods of classrooms there are outdoor patios of various scales into which the rock formations enter directly. Each of these outdoor spaces has its own unique qualities. In the smallest of these spaces a fragrance garden has been developed. In this case, there is also significant topographic displacement between adjacent pods, which further qualifies the space in between them.

In terms of the constructional syntax within the school, the long-span elements are all recycled steel, which is very efficient for long spans, while the rest of the structure is conventional wood framing, the predominant building technique of the region. Where there is human contact with this rather rough and robust construction, acoustic paneling and millwork softens it. Ramps and stairs mediate the transition between the adjacent teaching pods. In 1992 computers were just being introduced to elementary schools. So there was one computer pod rather than computers in all of the classrooms. In the area adjacent to the library, where there is the largest disjunction between adjacent pods, we created a reading nook, a storytelling area for the students.

The existing topography is used to advantage. In section the seating area adjacent to the basketball and volleyball court is provided by the change in elevation as one passes from the circulation spine to the gymnasium. Within the classrooms, we wanted to make sure that the students would not be overwhelmed by the language of the architecture. A skylight brings light deep into the core of the school and to the classrooms finished in drywall and painted white. In these spaces luminosity, in particular natural lighting, is very important, hence the surfaces are reflective and luminous. Light is brought in through clerestories. The architecture stands back at a point to provide planar surfaces for students to pin up their work. Even the most intimate parts of the classroom have views into social spaces and the adjacent classrooms. There is a sense of community in the school that goes beyond the individual classroom. In the design of the school, the social objective is as strong a motivation as issues of formal order and sustainability objectives. The budget allotted was the same as for any public school in British Columbia, and the tectonic language of the construction was achieved primarily because we were able to strip away many components of conventional construction.

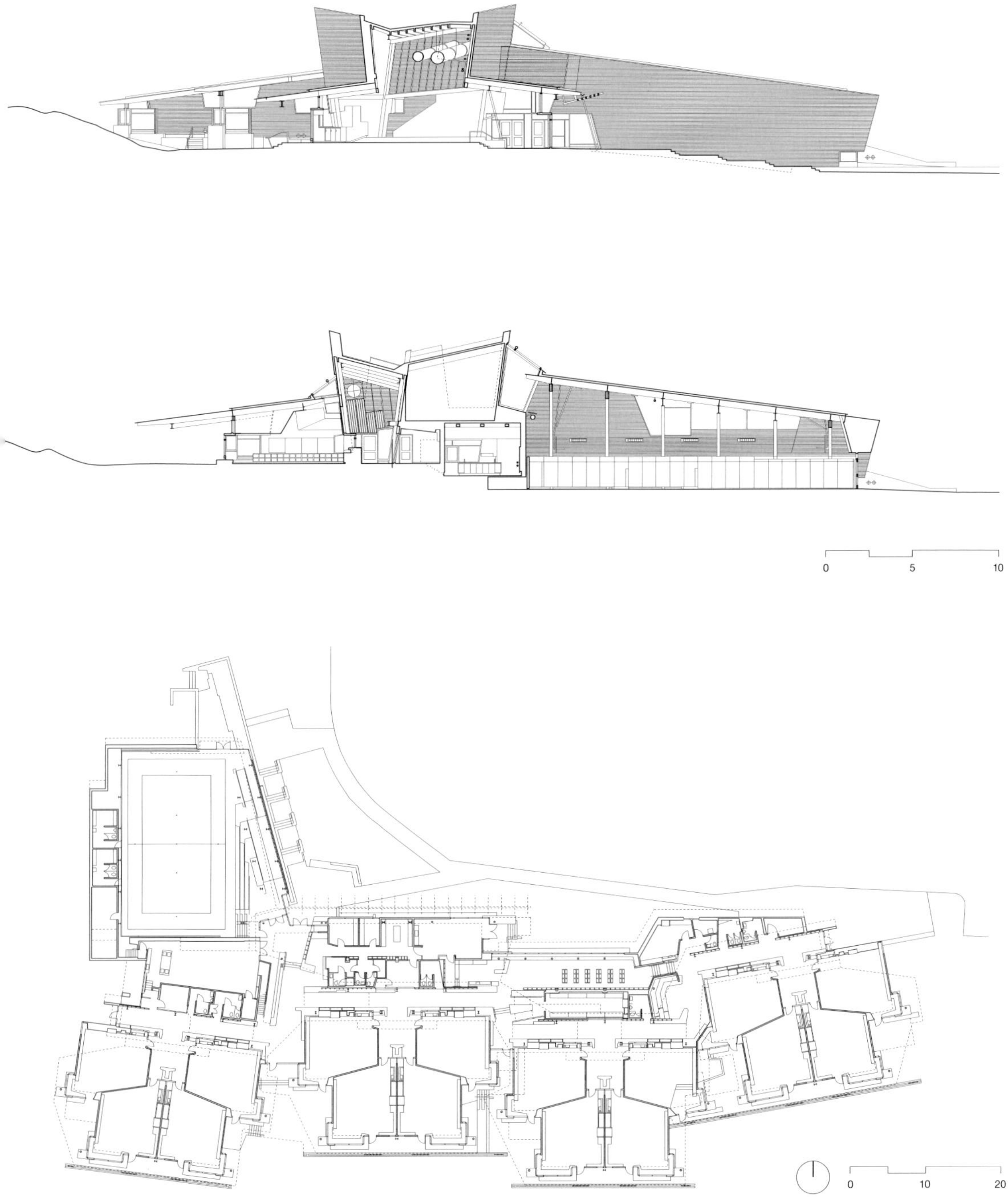

Strawberry Vale School. Top and center: Cross sections revealing spine of the building.
Bottom: Ground floor plan indicating the four classroom clusters with alternating play terraces

Strawberry Vale School. View through the library and the steel-framed spine of the building

Typical classroom interior

Interior view of the gymnasium

Strawberry Vale School. A typical shared outdoor teaching terrace with micro-landscape beyond

Grande Bibliothèque du Québec
Montreal, Québec, Canada, 2000–2005

This library, the largest publically accessible library in the French-speaking world, is 400,000 square feet (37,161 square meters), and located in the Latin Quarter of Montreal, an area inhabited by a diverse population. The site is located at a strategic intersection of three subway lines. It is a particularly appropriate location for the first large public library in the province of Québec.

In Montreal, as in all cities, the ground plane is an important public arena but here the city subway system has also evolved over the years into a world of its own. Thus there are significant facilities such as restaurants and shops that exist within a large and entirely subterranean network. We wanted to try to tie the library to both levels of this public realm. The first move was simply to make a direct connection between the subway and the library. One of the real challenges of large libraries is that because of the need to control access and the flow of books, there is a marked tendency to provide a rather enclosed building. As a result, libraries tend to have a single point of entrance, which can be very destructive from the point of view of their urban context.

To deal with this issue we developed a plan in which there were connections from a lane called Avenue Savoie going through to Rue Saint-Denis, which is a very important and lively street. We made connections to the Boulevard de Maisonneuve, a major cross-town access, and along Rue Berri in order to create a large public space.

The building is tied to its context. We listed all components of the program that could exist outside the domain of library control, such as the auditorium, some meeting rooms, the exhibition space, the shop, restaurants, a café, and a series of "bouquinistes,"—secondhand booksellers located along Avenue Savoie—which we redeveloped into a pedestrian lane.

Grande Bibliothèque du Québec, Montréal, QC, 2000–2005. Aerial view of the library in relation to the city of Montréal

Main entry portico to the library

Another unusual aspect to this project is the fact that there are two major collections housed within: a general one surrounded by reading rooms and another called the Collection Québécoise which is an archival library. It is like having two yolks in one egg. In response to that, we constructed two wooden envelopes housing the two collections within the larger envelope of the building. In addition to the interior circulation systems with which both of these libraries are served, we have developed a series of terraced spaces that act as access, reading room, and secondary route to complement the centralized circulation in the middle of each plan. Moving past the control checkpoint, one can take a long ramp up to the entrance of the Collection Québécoise or proceed on up a progressively stepped reading room that culminates in a space overlooking Avenue Savoie or take another stepped reading room to the uppermost one overlooking Rue Berri.

Coming from Vancouver, we were not familiar with the ability of local industry to custom-fabricate architectural components. This building is incredibly inexpensive. We completed it in 2005 at the rate of $110 per square foot (ca. $1,185 per square meter). The project managers deserve most of the credit. One of the virtues is that it is a very large building and there are certain economies that result from its sheer size. We went through an unbelievably rigorous value-engineering process at every stage of the project. The process involved the entire consultant team meeting with a complementary group of professionals, architects. and engineers and collaborating so as to eliminate every screw and rivet that was unnecessary.

The most interesting dimension of how we accomplished this building for so little money was that Québec has a remarkable infrastructure of fabricators. For example, much of the curtain wall constructed in New York City in recent years comes from Québec because there was an industry there with lower labor costs. Because of the ability to make things locally even the channel glass used in the project was made in Québec. This was the key to our ability to make what does not appear to be a cheap building with very little money. Subsequently we did another large library in another part of Canada and found that the opposite applied. In the Montreal library every component was custom-made whereas for the other library that we designed in Winnipeg we were not able to customize anything. Everything had to come from a catalogue because there was no infrastructure for the fabrication of components in that community. In this regard, there is a significant difference between the east and the west in Canada.

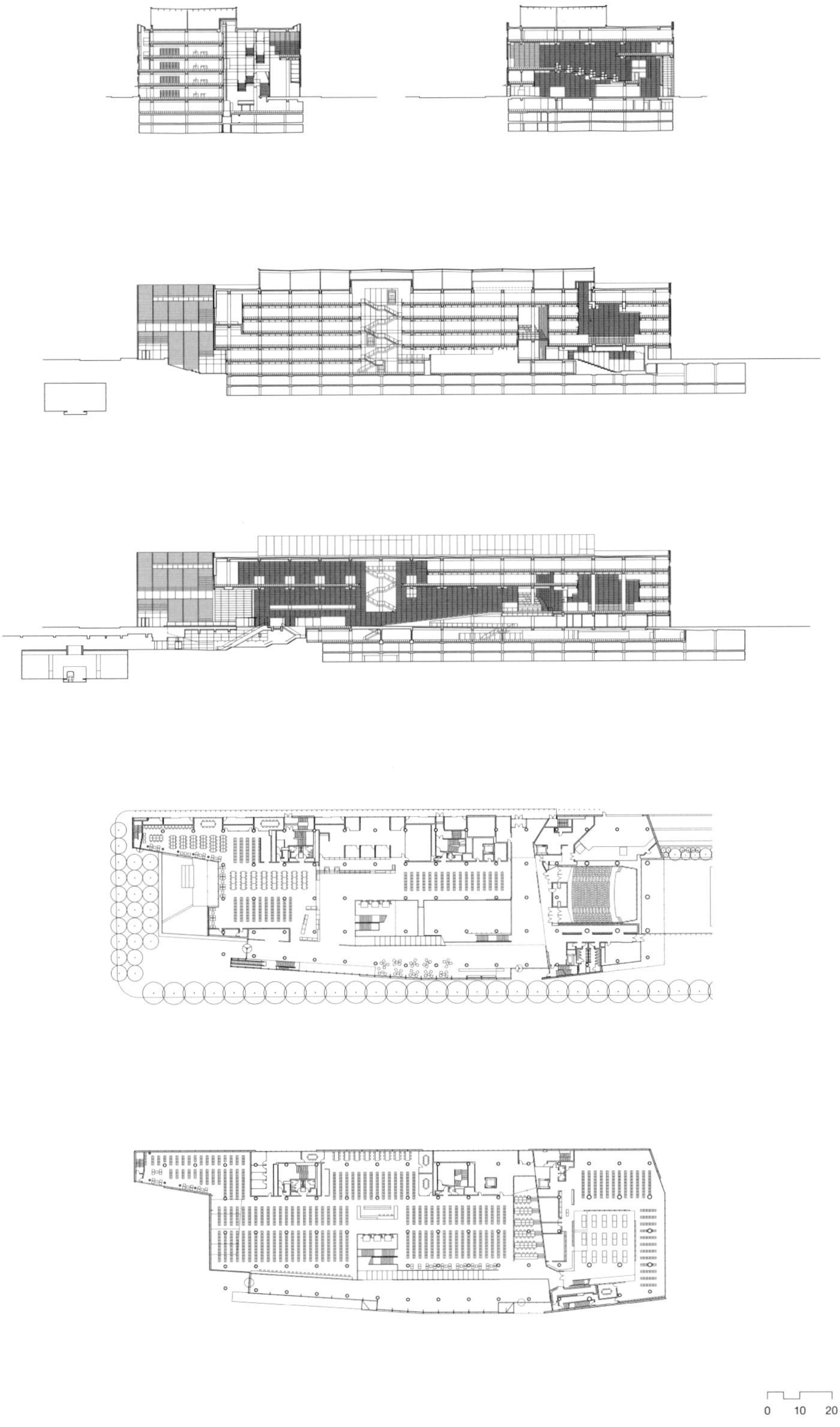

Grande Bibliothèque du Québec. Top to bottom: Transverse and longitudinal sections; ground floor plan; upper floor plan

Grande Bibliothèque du Québec. Clockwise from top: Main entry hall, enclosed with glass on one side and wood louvers on the other; the Québécoise library; one of two stepped reading rooms

View of the central suspended stairway system

Grande Bibliothèque du Québec. View of the alley behind library; a traditional venue for secondhand booksellers

Linear House
Salt Spring Island, British Columbia, Canada, 2006–2009

Our office occasionally designs houses, when we find a compatible client. We actually interview our house clients while they are interviewing us. This proviso is of consequence. Given the amount of energy you spend doing a house, it has to have some positive outcome for the office.

This project is a combined house and guesthouse, small in actual area but with a dimensional grandness. Grandness in this situation is created by both the unusual length of the plan and the short, high cross section. These two stretched dimensions make the house and guesthouse seem much bigger than their square footage —3,500 square feet (325 square meters)—suggest.

The project is situated on Salt Spring Island, one of the Gulf islands between Vancouver Island and the mainland of British Columbia. Salt Spring is an island full of small farms and great cheese makers. The site itself is a small 16-acre working farm. It is a site that has been lived on over time and added to by various owners, resulting in a strange diversity of attributes. It has a long entrance drive lined with fruit trees that leads to an old barn. It has a whole collection of strangely positioned, non-native tree species. There is a line of deformed mature cedars that ends the entrance drive. There is a row of huge fir trees splitting the property in two with a gap between the firs at one point that provides a view to the inter-island waterways and the next island. There are existing cane gardens and the remnants of an old orchard as well as working hay fields. The property included a collection of existing buildings: a cottage, a studio-guesthouse, garage, and barn. The owners are a couple who decided to retire to Salt Spring Island to enjoy island life. They had bought the land and at the time were living in the small cottage. We decided to keep all farm-related buildings. The cottage was sold, loaded, onto a trailer and moved down the road where it now provides accommodation for another family.

The clients both love food—cooking, baking, foraging, and growing it. They hunt, slaughter, and hang their own game. The initial program included a room in the house for hanging game upside down with cans to catch dripping blood. (We encouraged them to move this particular activity to the barn.) They enjoy the social aspects of cooking and gathering for meals with family and friends.

We wanted to build in a manner that would preserve the land's productivity. The land underneath and alongside the fir trees where the fir needles drop is some of the least productive land. We decided to build on this strip of land. We identified a long and narrow footprint of non-productive land, 370 feet (112.8 m) long and 33 feet (10.1 m) wide, which we understood as the site of the house. We thought of the rest of the landscape as something that could be repaired, augmented, and reinforced. We used the house site itself to separate out the fir trees from the rest of the landscape. The long dimension of the house faces north–south. One of our first considerations was to cut the length of the virtual building into two parts with a breezeway linking north site to south site, marking the view to the inter-island waterway at the cut, and separating a guesthouse from the main house. Then

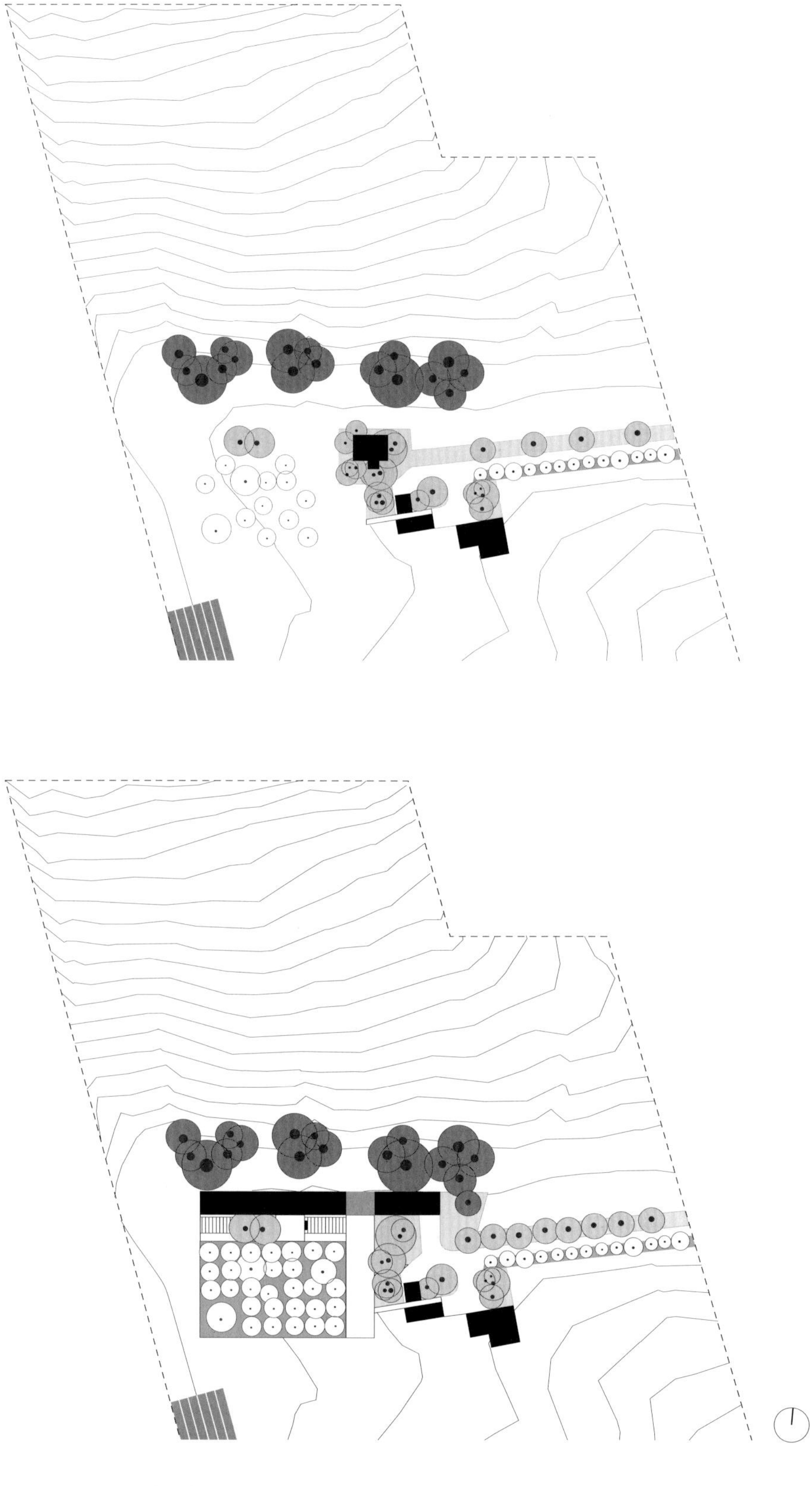

Linear House, Salt Spring Island, BC, 2006–2009. Before and after site plans of the farmstead with the house and garden positioned against a line of fir trees

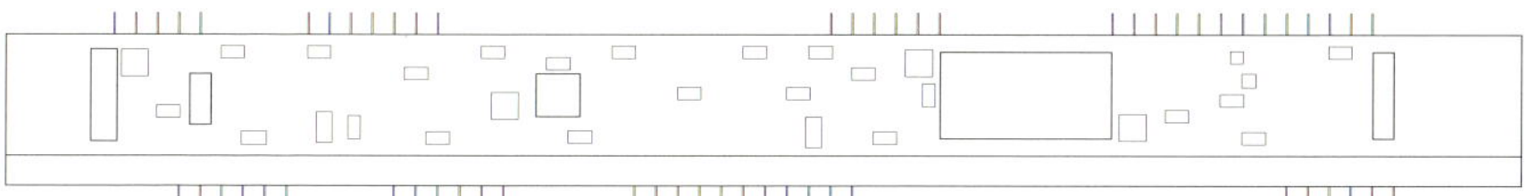

Roof Plan

Reflected Ceiling Plan

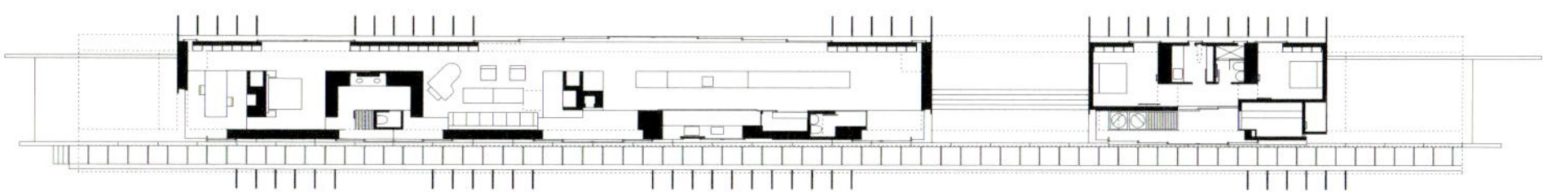

Floor Plan

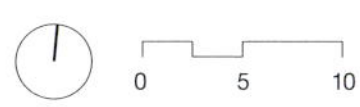

Top: View of the farmstead before construction, and close-up of the Linear House in position
Bottom: Plans showing skylights, structural grid, and basic layout

we started to think about an inside-outside condition for the house, a condition that might start to evoke an architecture. We thought about the outside as fairly solid, dense, and recessive and the inside as luminous, full of light. We held the interior envelopes in from either end to provide a covered car park at one end and a covered terrace at the other. Interiors were considered as primary volumes of luminous space that would be modulated by two fireplace concrete cores and then augmented with a series of service cores such as washrooms, closets, wine storage, and the like. We then scattered about 40 skylights of different sizes over the roof. The skylights are of two types: they are either operable for both daylight and cross-ventilation or inoperable and simple daylighting devices.

The main house has a straightforward plan with a very long communal kitchen and dining space adjacent to a fireplace/baking core. The messy part of the kitchen can be closed off while dining or opened to enlarge work space. The fireplace/baking core separates the kitchen from a relatively small living area. A service area housing the master bathroom and closet separates the living room from the master bedroom and a small study. Sliding glazed doors on either side of the main house bar can be opened to create clear spans of up to 80 feet (24.4 m). In good weather, the house becomes redefined as an open shelter continuous with the spaces of its site. The guesthouse includes a sauna, cold plunges, washroom, two small bedrooms, and a laundry. Again, banks of sliding doors open to make both sauna and plunges continuous with the site. The building is wood-frame construction and employs giant wooden box beams to span major openings and to form cantilevers. The walls are load bearing.

Four kinds of depth affected the development of the house—site depth, surface depth, zonal depth, and phenomenal depth.

The siting of the house produces the greatest experiential depth possible on the site. By pressing the house tight against the fir trees, you can actually see through the fir trees. The perceptual depth produced therefore stretches between the experiential boundaries of the property, from the distant inter-island condition on the north to a line of fir trees at the southernmost periphery of the site. If we had sited the house anywhere else, the apparent depth of the site would have been reduced because of an inability to see through the line of fir trees from any distance. You would have lost this expansiveness of site depth.

Surface depth arises from the idea of extended thresholds. This is a very skinny house, but one that nevertheless has cross-sectional depth, produced in part by casework and bookshelves lining the walls. In other places the depth of the wall expands to accommodate the stack space for the 80 feet (24.4 m) of sliding doors. Beyond this stacking space, four-foot-deep (1.2 m) cementitious panels, placed perpendicular to the length of the house, further extend the threshold at openings. The combination of casework, stacking space and cement panels produce a perceived interior/exterior threshold measuring over seven feet (2.1 m) in places.

Zonal depth operates simply as certain service areas, such as the skinny "messy" kitchen that opens or closes to recalculate the apparent dimensions of interior volumes.

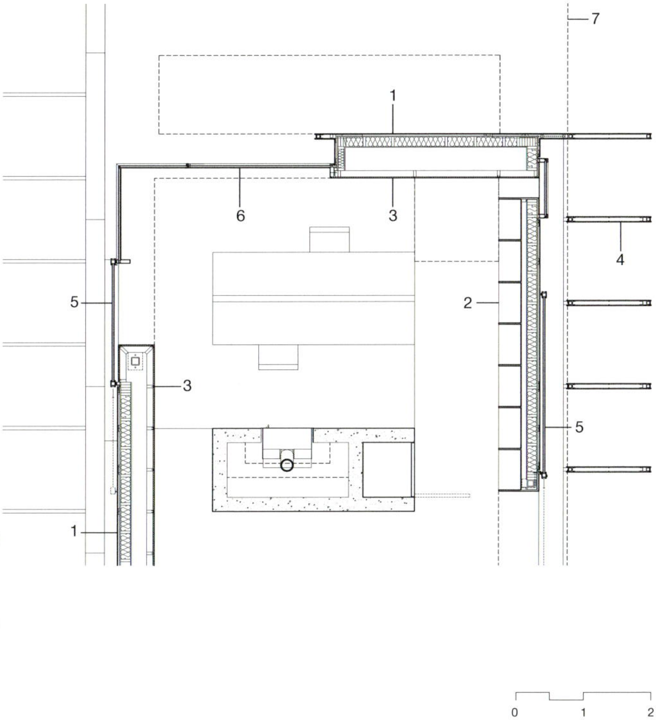

1 Cement board panel
2 Hardwood-veneer shelving unit
3 Translucent double-skin acrylic panel
4 Cement board "fin"
5 Top-hung double-glazed aluminum sliding doors
6 Double-glazed aluminum curtain wall
7 Roofline

Linear House, Salt Spring Island, BC. Top: Side view of house
Bottom: Horizontal constructional section showing the fins that modulate the mass of the house

Linear House, Top Left: View of the house framing a vista beneath the line of trees

1 2 ply SBS roof membrane
2 3/8" cement board panel
3 3/8" cement board 'fin' each side 2 × 2 galv HSS steel frame
4 Top-hung double-glazed aluminum sliding doors
5 site finished laminated hardwood floor 8" cantilevered concrete slab c/w cast-in radiant heating
6 2" exposed concrete topping with cast-in radiant heating
7 compact fluorescent light fixture
8 translucent double-skin acrylic panel

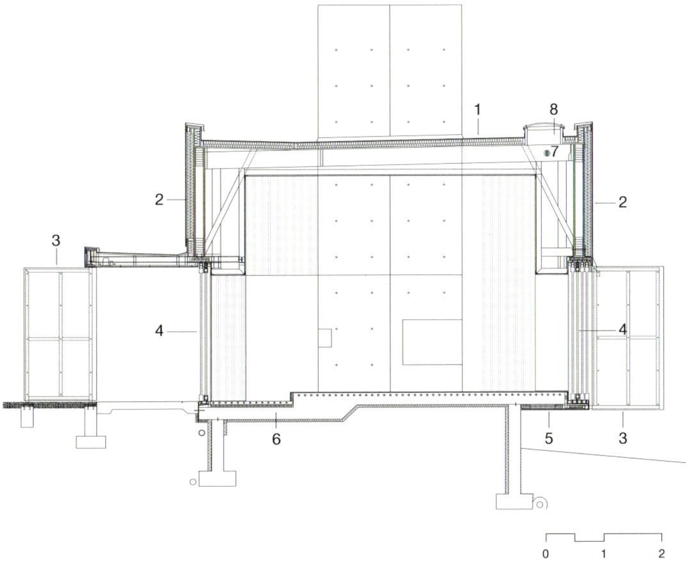

Cross section showing construction details

Overall view of house as a continuous section

Linear House, clockwise from top: View from kitchen and dining area, exterior glazing fully retracted; guest quarters bedroom plus view of master bedroom shower with exterior glazing retracted

Phenomenal depth in the project arises from a constructional idea. We used traditional stick framing to produce a double surface in the project, with a space of about 16 inches (41 cm) between layers. The exterior layer is the actual envelope while the interior surface is a daylight dispersion layer skinned with translucent cellular acrylic panels. Over 40 skylights were then "sprinkled" over the roof plane, drawing daylight into or through the interstitial zone between inside and outside skins. Certain skylights puncture the layered zone, bringing light into the interior. Other smaller ones transfer light into the space between layers dispersing light along the plastic skin. Some shafts of light come in directly, like those seen piercing dense forests, while others are transferred around edges, eating away the apparent volumes. What results is an ineffable surface of luminous depth, a surface that changes constantly with climate and daily and seasonal cycles. The Linear House produces an everchanging light much like that of our native forests. The visual press of the line of fir trees on space and the ineffability of the "forest" light act together to situate space strangely, both in this place and out of it simultaneously.

On the outside, the house has an almost dappled elephantine character. The soft black cementitious board takes on a subtly changing reflected glow, according to exterior conditions, looking sometimes almost purple or deep brown and sometimes pure black. The exterior surface quietly transforms itself according to the light that falls on it while within, the house has phenomenal depths of luminous interiority.

Another consideration was the craft of the detail. There are significant challenges to building on islands because, unless there is a huge budget, trades cannot be brought in. The idea of craft needs to account for this. Our response was to use two different kinds of pre-manufactured, dimensionally repetitive, material panels to give scale and control to surfaces. The exterior Swiss Pearl fiber cement panel is strong and thin. Exterior "fins" can therefore be thin as well, two panels attached to either side of slender metal frames. The impermeability of the exterior panel eliminates the necessity for flashing along with the flashing joints, which, in a wet climate, can cause irregular surface staining on walls.

This project inserts itself carefully into agricultural land. The construction of the building does not diminish productive land. The design attempts to make sense of a disparate set of conditions, none of which are spectacular in any way, and all of which construct the opportunities and the "sense" of a richly diversified small farm. This project describes a form of shelter that allows its occupants to live differently from season to season, adjusting to the desire for different temperatures, degrees of enclosure, and connection across boundaries as time passes.

Increasingly, we think of our work as a project of trying to establish relationships between things, a means of constructing mutually beneficial ground between the circumstances of the project, enduring natural systems, and the needs and desires of individual clients and communities.

Steven Holl

Steven Holl was born in 1947 in Bremerton, Washington. He graduated from the University of Washington and pursued architecture studies in Rome in 1970. In 1976, he attended the Architectural Association in London and established Steven Holl Architects in New York City.

Steven Holl has realized cultural, civic, academic, and residential projects both in the United States and internationally. Notable work includes the Kiasma Museum of Contemporary Art in Helsinki, Finland (1998), the Chapel of St. Ignatius, Seattle, Washington (1997), and the Nelson-Atkins Museum of Art (2007). The Cité de l'Océan et du Surf Museum, a collaboration with Solange Fabião, opened in Biarritz, France, on June 26, 2011, and the Nanjing Museum of Art and Architecture in China will open in November 2011. Currently in design are the Glasgow School of Art, the new University of Iowa Arts Building, and the Princeton University Center of Creative and Performing Arts. Under construction are the large mixed-use Sliced Porosity Block in Chengdu, China, a private residence and art gallery in Seoul, Korea, and the Beirut Marina and Town Quay.

Steven Holl is a professor at Columbia University's Graduate School of Architecture, Planning and Preservation.

Steven Holl
Rule and Exception

I want to begin by with an anecdote about how important Kenneth Frampton's *Modern Architecture: A Critical History* was in the 1980s. Dimitra Tsachrelia in my office reminded me of just how many languages the book has been translated into. She told a story about when she was in studying in Greece; the book was in every school and when the students misplaced their copy, they would ask each other, "Where's my Frampton, where's my Frampton?" For a long time, she thought that "Frampton" meant book. She didn't realize that Frampton was a person.

I grew up in Seattle and early in my career I went to San Francisco for an internship. I met Stanley Saitowitz, Mark Mack, and William Stout reading amazing texts in *Oppositions*. Most of all, I was drawn to Kenneth's texts. Peter Eisenman was always a shock, but Kenneth's texts were polemical and engaging. When I came to New York in 1974—at the time I had a beard like a San Francisco hippie—I occasionally audited his lectures at Columbia and sat in the back. I remember Kenneth was giving a lecture about Le Corbusier and some of his early houses, and I was struck by his amazing enthusiasm not just for the figure of Le Corbusier, but for architecture. After the lecture, I followed his class to the Symposium Restaurant, which is still there, just a few blocks from Columbia. I snuck into the restaurant and sat listening, perhaps a little too obviously. At one point Kenneth said, "Well, come over and join us if you like." He always radiated this enthusiasm and generosity.

For this event, I have elected to posit five axioms in his honor:

1. Site: Architecture is bound to situation; it is architecture's physical and metaphysical foundation. (I realize that my first book, *Anchoring,* was influenced by Kenneth's essays on critical regionalism.)
2. Structure: If structure is often 25 percent of the cost of a building, it must be integral to its meaning. I have followed that principle in my work. (I always think I will invite Kenneth to come see a building and show him some piece of the structure.)
3. Spatial energy: Perception develops from a series of overlapping perspectives of the body in space.
4. Light: Luminosity equals consciousness. Space is oblivion without light.
5. The haptic realm: Materiality and psychological dimensions are engaged.

School of Art and Art History
University of Iowa, Iowa City, Iowa, 2006

Extending the studio space and library of the University of Iowa's School of Art and Art History was an interesting project but it was not an interesting site. It was an open field, flanked by an abandoned quarry pond. We built several test models, including one of Le Corbusier's Carpenter Center for the Visual Arts, which has the same size and program. The field site was boring; instead we decided to engage with the quarry pond as our site. The physical plant department of the university said, "You can't. It's impossible. You'll never fit the program on the other side of that utility line." For economy, we chose to use an exposed steel-frame structure. This meant that the building could not go higher than two-and-a-half floors. However, what we could do was to cantilever part of the library out over the pond, allowing us to hold the utility line and thereby save the field site.

They came to my office and said, "Steven, you're not really trying to build it over the pond, are you?" and I responded, "If we build over the pond, you can save the rest of the site, you can build a new building on it. That site is probably worth five million dollars." This was the argument that sold the scheme in the end. The building is a planar construction with a part of the library pushed out over the pond. We made a model in steel with Guy Nordenson, who engineered the structure. We developed a series of model studies over a period of six months. At a certain moment, the design seemed to look a little like Picasso's *Guitar* of 1912. Given that this was an art department, they loved the analogy. In total, we added 70,000 square feet (6,500 square meters) to the school and saved the site the University originally wanted to use. All the elements, including the steel, were exposed and we did not have to use fireproofing

School of Art and Art History, Iowa City, IA, 2006. Site model

because of the two-and-a-half-story rule. Chris McVoy, my partner, figured out how to not have any ductwork and to run all the air through the hollow cores of the precast concrete planks. All the details of these edge conditions were studied first in watercolors and then converted to working drawings.

There was a "Percent for Art" commission for the building, and the wonderful artist Richard Artschwager came to my studio to discuss the project. In a way he had a premonition about what would happen to this project in its near future. He talked about a sitting figure, like those Egyptian figures that had to be moved when they flooded the Nile for the Aswan Dam in the seventies. He created a similar sculpture at three times life size, whose feet just touched the pond. The pond is part of the university experience now with a deck where the students can walk. There are dormitories at the back, so the students can thread their way through the building and thereby make it part of the campus space.

The main entrance has a gallery that exhibits students' work. The exit stairs are of planar construction and there is plywood lining in the hallways and the classrooms. The library opens up into two parts: half in the bridge, half in the main structure. We suspended a stair fabricated out of sheet steel, which serves as an integral part of the structure. This stairway has become a gathering place in the school. People from other departments in the university are using the library and it has become a general meeting place.

We used raw concrete with a terrazzo grinder run over it for the floor. Using terrazzo would have cost sixteen dollars a square foot (ca. $172 a square meter) whereas terrazzo-ground concrete was only four dollars a square foot (ca. $43 a square meter). A very tight budget does not mean you have to sacrifice spatial energy. The studios, for instance, are at the very top, crowning the building. We oriented them to get north light, thinking of Brancusi's studio. Altogether, the planarity of the building creates a condition of fuzzy edges and we thought of these edges as the interface between art and architecture.

Global warming is real, even if it is contrary to what half of the recently elected members of Congress believe. The Iowa River flooded in the spring of 2008 with a flood level that is only supposed to occur every five hundred years. Luckily, we had the library up in the air. The flood, which put 16 buildings under water, basically transformed the campus. The Federal Emergency Management Agency (FEMA) has been in there now and finally this building has been refurbished. Unfortunately, the original 1937 building will not be rebuilt. We won a competition in February 2010, which means that we are now designing the replacement of the 1937 building, which we originally added to—an odd condition. Because of the new flood level the original field site will always remain empty as a campus green. Our new building will be based on making light structure employing similar geometry.

School of Art and Art History. Site plan showing the location of the building next to lake

View from the northeast

Early watercolor of a central steel staircase

View of the realized construction

School of Art and Art History. View from the south

Nelson-Atkins Museum of Art
Kansas City, Missouri, 2007

The most specific instruction for the six architects competing for the addition to the Nelson-Atkins Museum of Art was to add on to the north side of the existing museum. We were not supposed to go down into the landscape. All the competitors were very obedient and followed the stipulated conditions. But I thought it was terrible to block the north facade of this 1937 building. We wanted to do something more idealistic and make a contrast by merging the building into the landscape. The metaphorical concept was that if the original building was a stone, the new building would be a feather. The original building has directed circulation, and the addition was to have open circulation. The original building is inward looking, while the addition looks out into the landscape.

I got the courage to be disobedient and break the rules when I read an inscription in the original facade, "The soul has greater need of the ideal than of the real." During the competition presentation I also referred to a painting by Zhou Chen from 1536 called *The North Sea,* which is in the museum's collection. The Nelson-Atkins has an enormously interesting collection of Asian art. The painting fuses landscape and architecture, and I argued that we would try, in a new way, to make the addition fuse the landscape and the architecture.

In a series of drawings we studied the pavilions to see if we could use lenses to conduct light down into the gallery system below, and at the same time form not just an object but a spatial field. We wanted to leave the facades of the original building free. It gradually evolved into something like a 60-story skyscraper lying on its side underground, a volume that was punctured with lenses to bring the light down inside.

The key to our success in the competition was connecting the addition to the original building. Chris McVoy figured out how we could remove one wall and create a perpendicular cross-link, beautifully linking all the galleries of the original building with the new, more freely organized circulation routes leading to the new galleries. The old building, which is 100,000 square feet larger (9,290 square meter) than the new one, feeds into the addition along a perpendicular axis.

The building was realized in phases. The parking garage and the infrastructure were first. To support the plaza and the artwork above the parking garage in front of the original building, we designed what were called "Wave Ts," special precast-concrete elements, each weighing 60,000 pounds. The superstructure consists of only Wave Ts and columns. An artwork by Walter De Maria, entitled, *One Sun/34 Moons,* contains openings that act as skylights, through which light descends to the parking garage below. Because there is water on top, the light ripples and moves, making up a permanent piece of art that cannot be disturbed in the future. Perhaps because of the height of the space and the quality of the light streaming in, the garage has been used as more than a parking place. People have even held picnics there, and when the museum was first built, a black-tie event was held in the garage.

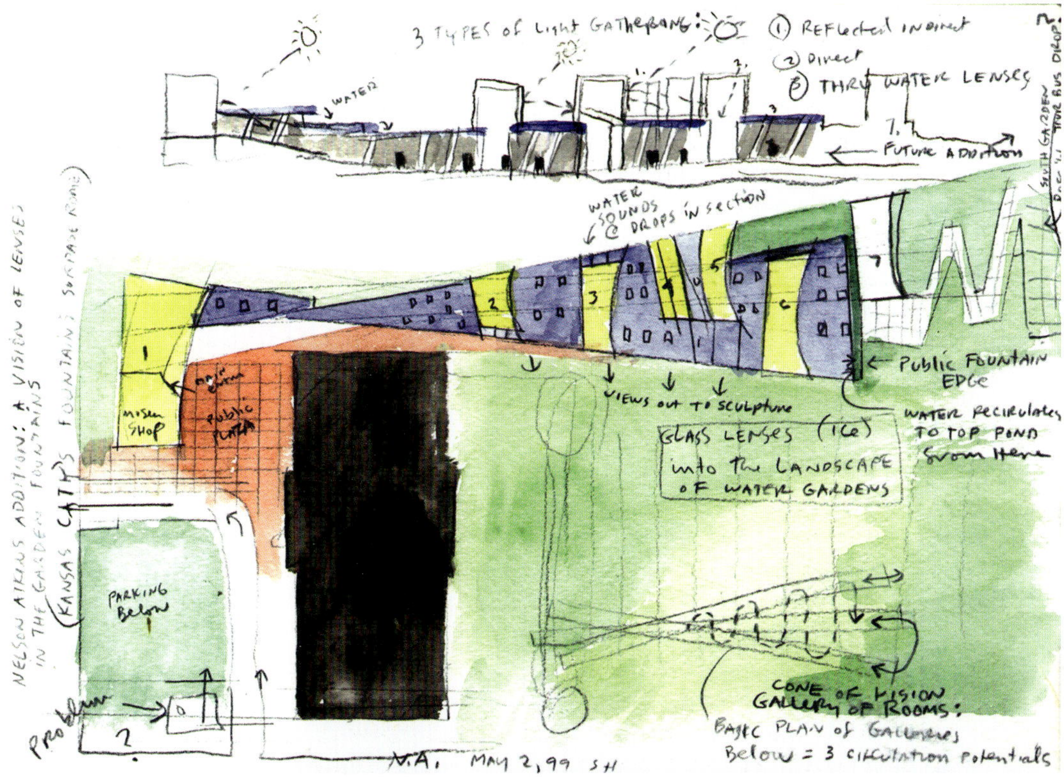

Early conceptual sketch of the Nelson-Atkins Museum of Art, Kansas City, MO, 2007

View of the completed building at night

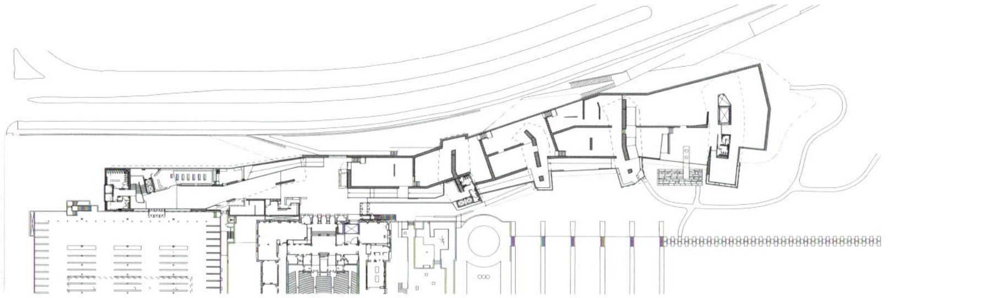

Ground floor plan

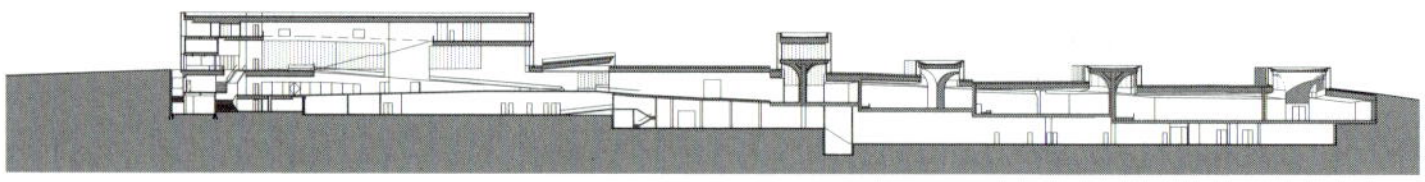

Longitudinal section

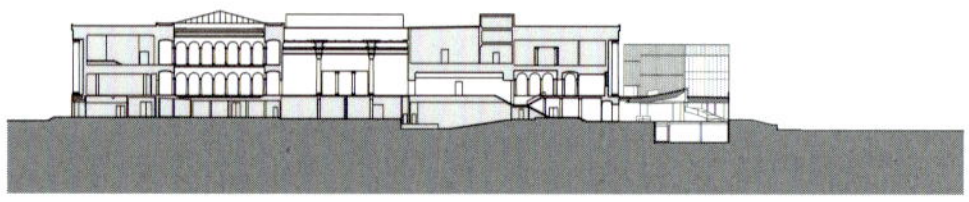

Cross section: lower lobby and original building through cross axis

Nelson-Atkins Museum of Art, Plan of gallery level; Longitudinal and cross sections

View of the main staircase

View of the reflecting pool in front of the Bloch Building, with Walter de Maria's *One Sun/34 Moons*, whose "moon" skylights penetrate the garage beneath.

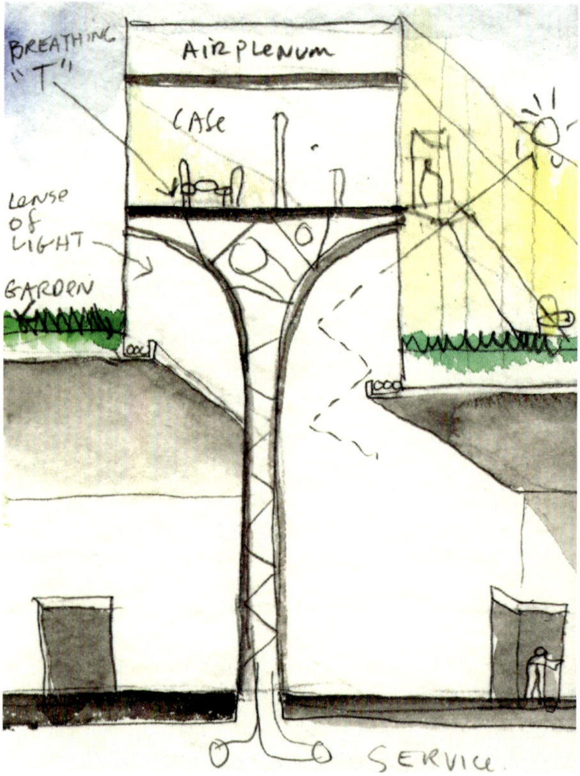

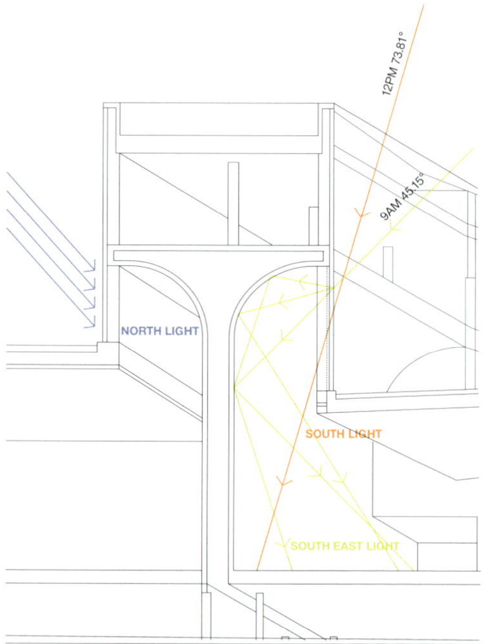

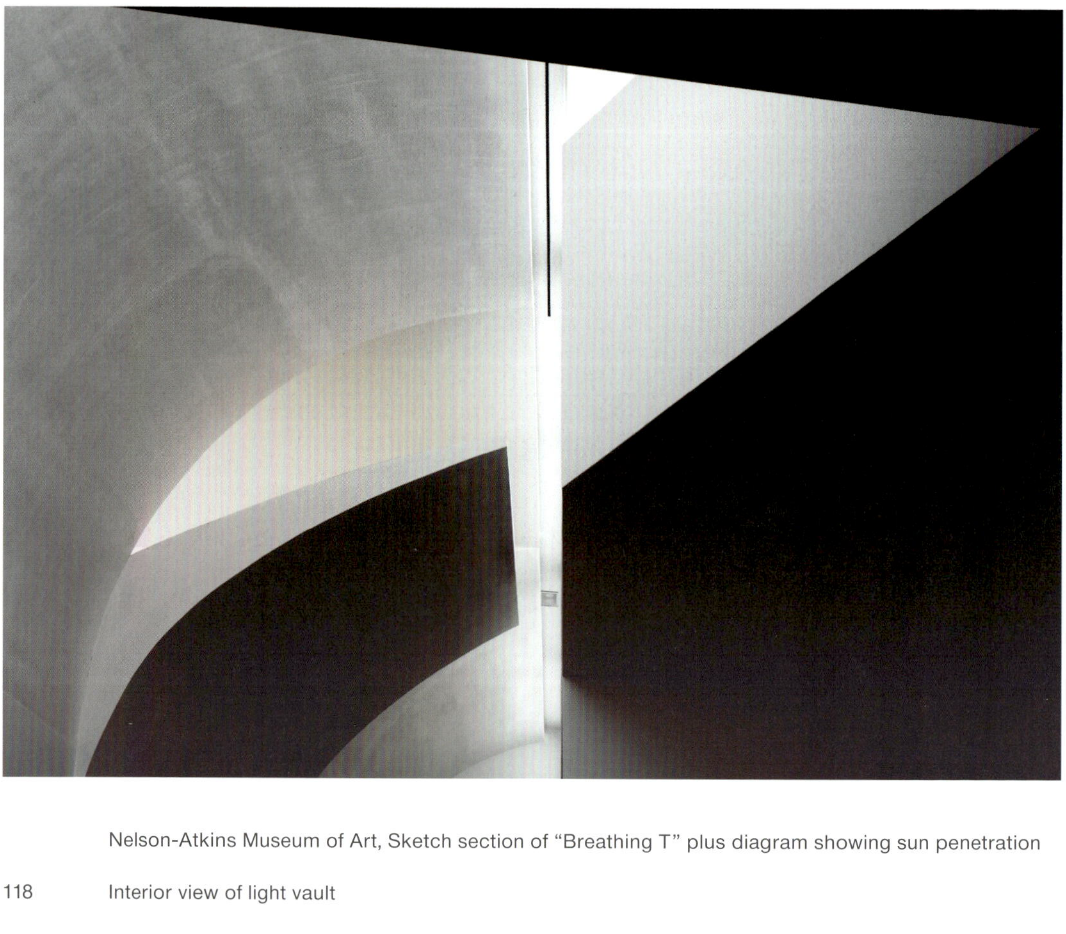

Nelson-Atkins Museum of Art, Sketch section of "Breathing T" plus diagram showing sun penetration

Interior view of light vault

Guy Nordenson, who engineered the stair at the University of Iowa School of Art and Art History, also designed the structure of the main stair in the Nelson-Atkins Museum. I wanted the stair to serve as a structural element, so we had to install this stair at the second level of the entrance pavilion before the other structure. It is painted conceal the steel but when one touches it, one realizes that it is a solid steel beam that one is walking on.

In addition to the Wave Ts used in the subterranean garage, there were what we called "Breathing Ts," concrete structures that allowed us to bring light down to the galleries, but which also served to support the structure and connect to the services below. These allowed for the merging of a unique light condition, with both the HVAC system and the structure. To get this solution to work took us around a year to develop. We were having a problem with the quality of the light. From the north, the light was too blue and from the south it was too warm. So we developed a notion of fluttering the shape of the Ts in certain places to mix the cool and warm light coming in from the north and south sides. Some of the "Breathing Ts" became "Fluttering Ts," a solution that subtly mixes the bluish light with the warm light.

The museum houses one of the largest collections of Isamu Noguchi's work in the Midwest. There was an idea to place an unfinished Noguchi out in the garden. During the competition we had the idea of using a work called *Fountain* and extending the piece out into the landscape. The building is open on all sides and one is free to enter at more than one point. I appreciate the efforts of the trustees for taking the opposite tack from the Museum of Modern Art by removing the entrance fee entirely rather than raising it. It is truly a public museum.

Experiencing the building outside feels like it is built out of blocks of light. When the sun goes down some rheostats turn the cavity lights on for the public space. People jog through here at night. The gardens are open at nights for the different activities that go on in Kansas City.

In achieving this effect, probably the most difficult technical aspect was the cavity wall, a glass wall whose cavity is large enough for people to walk around in. It also meant convincing the client to use a channel glass that was specially made in Germany. The glass was formed into 16-inch (41 cm) wide structural planks, spanning the optimum length. Each piece is German optical glass with no soda content, so that the glass is free of any green tint that might affect the light. The changes in the seasons are magnified by the combination of the pond and the way channel glass works. It can be a fantastic space even in freezing winter and different times of day and night.

This complex work was the ultimate result of an exceptional collaboration between Chris McVoy and Casey Cassias, along with a team of very dedicated people. I just do the watercolors.

Nelson-Atkins Museum of Art. Night view

Queens Community Library
Queens, New York, New York, Scheduled to begin in early 2012

This project has never been presented before. It is for a small, 20,000-square-foot (1,858 square meter) community library in Queens within a so-called hyper-development zone near Gantry Crane Park. It is surrounded by very large condominium towers, which are hardly a sympathetic context.

Instead, we looked to the Pepsi-Cola sign, the Gantry Cranes, and the sight of Long Island to serve as our context. There is also a wonderful relationship here between Louis Kahn's FDR Memorial, Oscar Niemeyer and Le Corbusier's UN Headquarters, the Pepsi-Cola sign, and our site. It is an amazingly charged site for a little building.

Right from the beginning, the clients wanted us to engage the Manhattan views. Secondly, we realized that the essence of a library today is to integrate digital media within a collective space carrying books. Thirdly, we wanted to indicate that this is a library with special spaces for children, teenagers, and adults.

The idea was to enter the library via a garden. The material of the building was to connect to its ecological meaning. In addition it should have an iconic presence so that one would be attracted to come there both from Queens and from across the river.

We worked on this building for four months. We could not show anybody because we did not believe we really had a scheme. Everything could be spread out on one level, and the site was big enough to accommodate the whole building in this manner. The site is 49,000 square feet (4,552 square meters) and the building is 21,000 square feet (1,951 square meters). We had to have an alternative argument. There must have been 2 different models on my table that we did not proceed with.

In the end, it was an idea about the view that carried the day. We created a cut in the facade that was connected to the idea of a browsing circuit, an idea that goes back to my design for the Amerika Gendenk-Bibliothek in Berlin built around a browsing circuit—the idea is that such a circuit would connect the entire building, right up to the roof garden. The facade would be sliced along the lines of movement, and indicate children's, adults' and teenagers' spaces.

In other words, there would be a connection between what this building looks like and how it is experienced. And the second thing, which I am very eager about, is finding a way to make books prominent. When I go into Rem Koolhaas's library in Seattle, everybody in the room is using a computer. You do not see a single book. I wanted to do something to register the presence of books; I think books will always be important. Thus we devised a scheme in which everybody can be on their computers and can also see Manhattan, but that still allows the visitor to be greeted on arrival by a lot of books. The space is really about the feeling of looking up and being able to see the books and the computers, making them all cohabit. The initial drawings were very small, but were worked over and over. The entire project came together very quickly after we had a concept that would tie everything together.

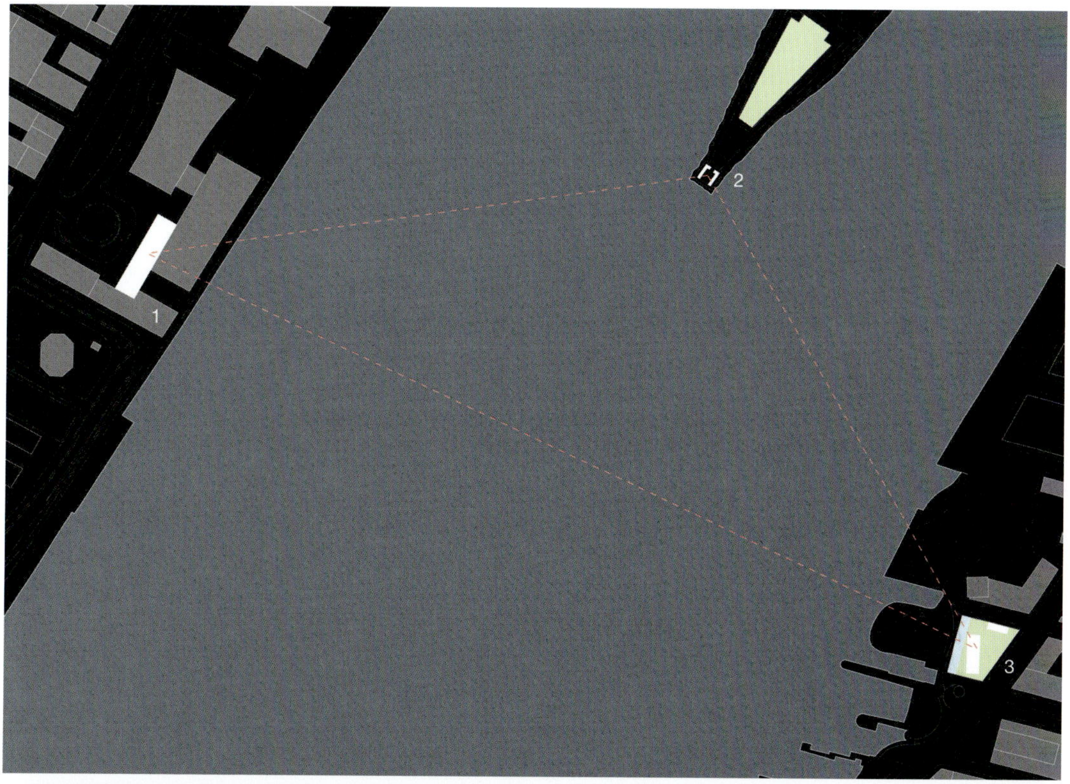

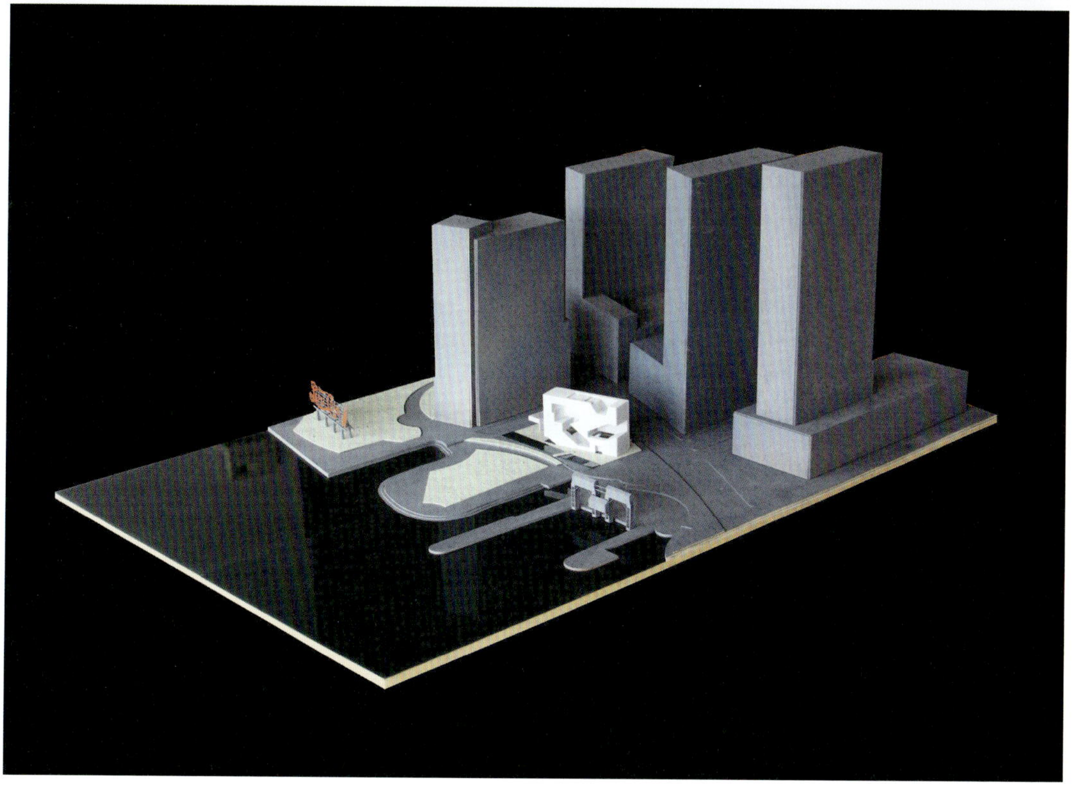

Map of the East River, New York; 1 UN headquarters, 2 Roosevelt Memorial, 3 Queens Community Library

The Queens Community Library, New York, NY, Site model of the library in context

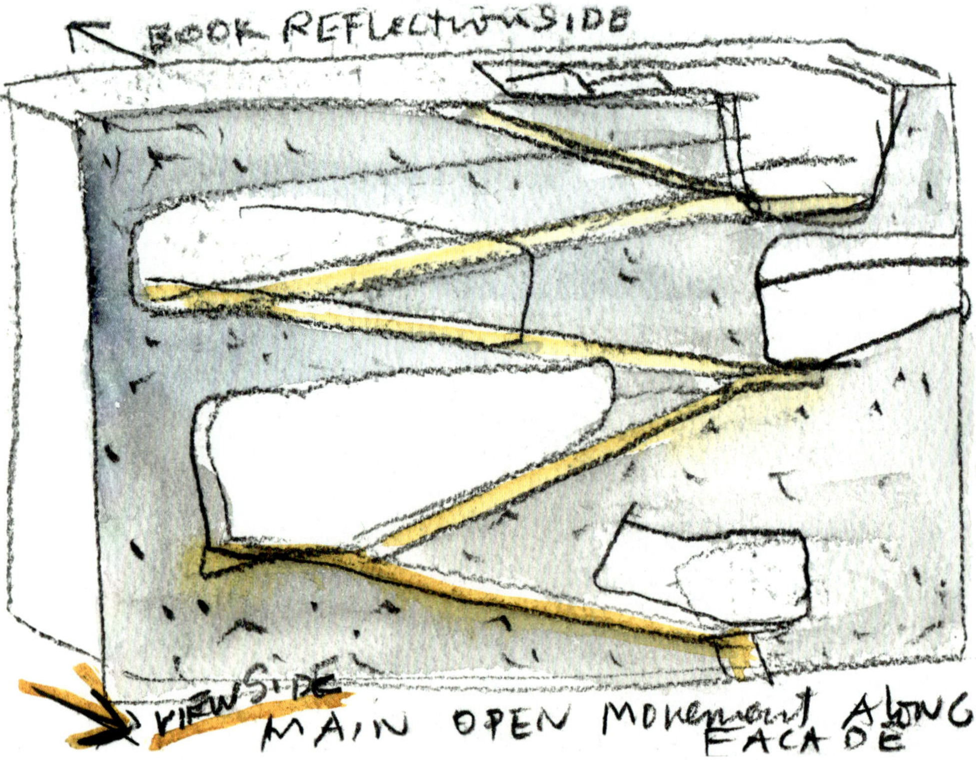

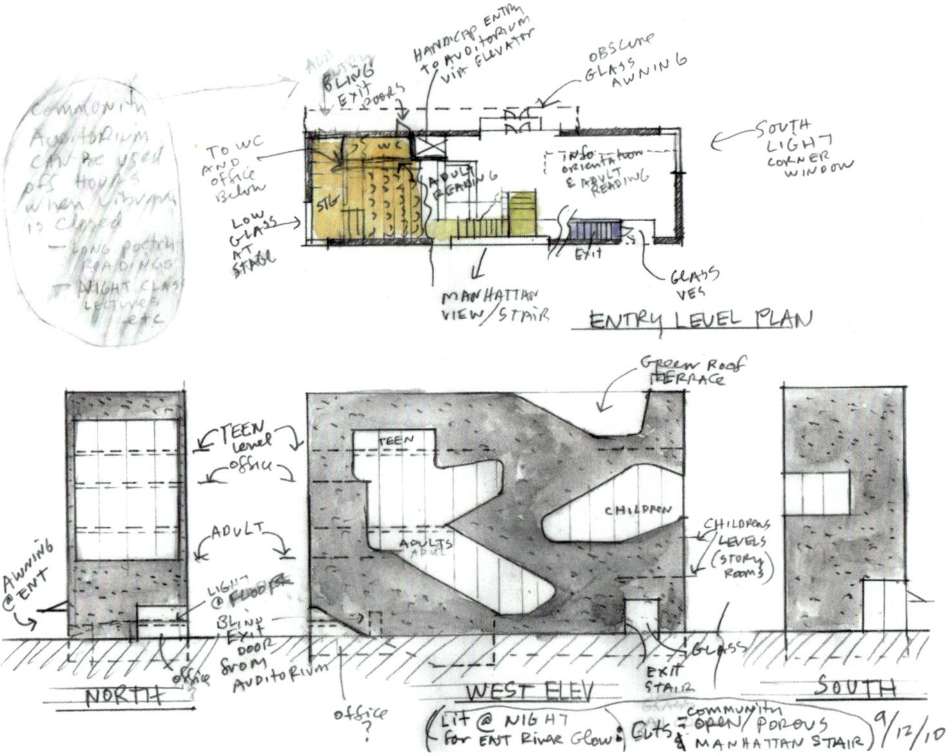

The Queens Community Library. Earlier sectional sketches of the library

Perspective of the stepped reading room with a large picture window overlooking the East River

Pepsi-Cola

Queens Community Library photomontaged against a backdrop of the Queens side of the East River

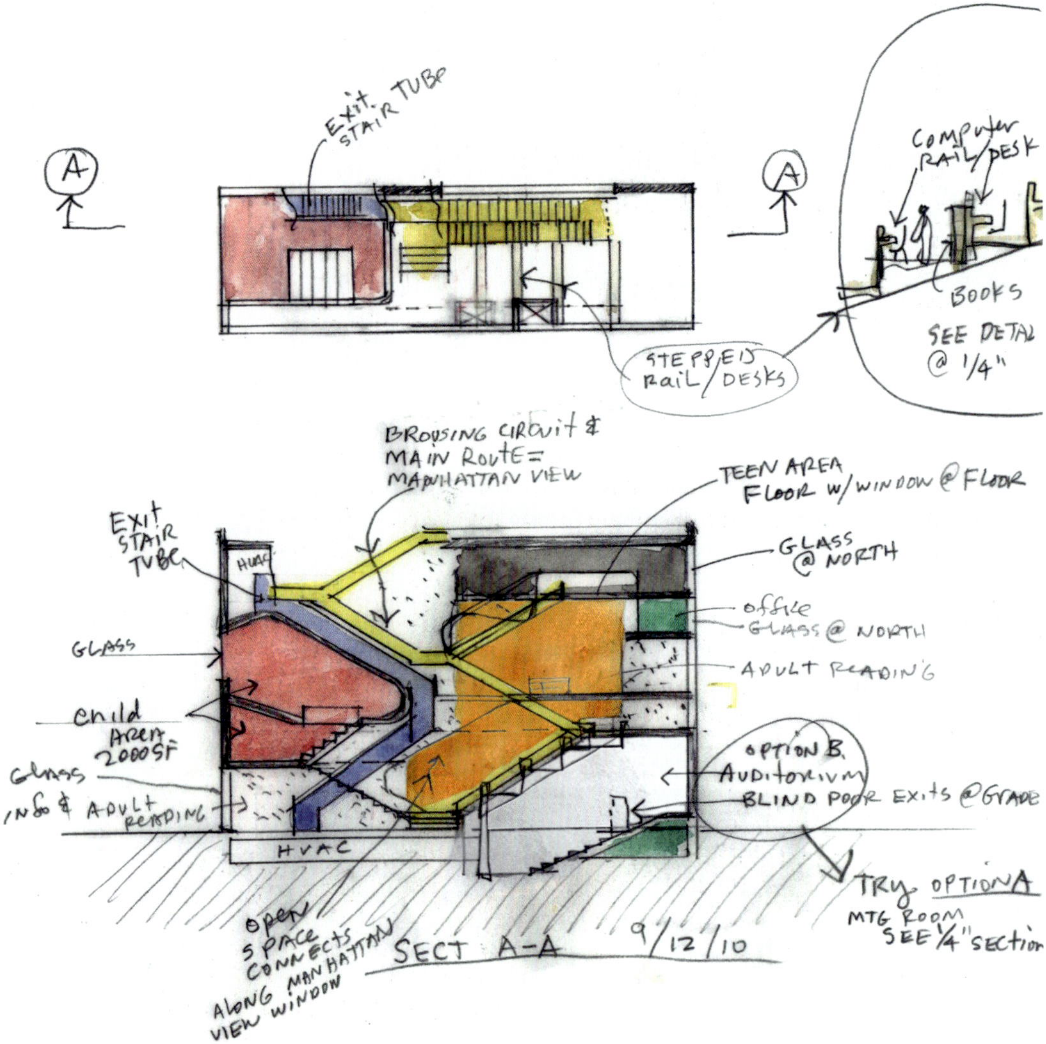

Early plan and section sketch indicating elements of program

The browsing circuit connects everything in the building all the way to the top, from the children's area to the adult section and the teen section at the top. You can read these three zones in the facade. The building will be 42 feet (12.8 m) wide with concrete bearing walls, allowing for a column-free space inside. Concrete wall insulation and recycled foamed aluminum make up the facade. I am very excited about this 80-foot-tall (24.4 m) building with its calligraphic cuts.

In the end, we did not want the project to have the quality of a big architectonic slab, so we turned the building to face west, creating a triangular entry garden. The garden gives public space back to the community. The garden, designed by landscape architect Michael Van Valkenburgh, has one entering the building through gingko trees.

To summarize, I knew this was going to be a Framptonian occasion, but I did not feel that others were also going to produce axioms. In fact, Lars Müller said, "Steven, don't you know, it's so out of style to do axioms?" and I replied, "What are you talking about, Lars?" He said, "Well, nobody talks like that. Nobody thinks like that anymore." I said, "Critique today is very sloppy." No one has clear statements about what they are doing. They talk about technique. I am not against the digital technique because digital technology is great, but if it is all about a euphoria of technique, it is a non-dialogue. I proposed 5 axioms in the spirit of dialogue and in honor of the great critical legacy of Kenneth Frampton's teaching.

View of the model in Holl's office poised on top of Umberto Eco's *In the Name of the Rose*

Project Credits: Five North American Architects

Stanley Saitowitz

Yerba Buena Lofts
Location: San Francisco, California, USA
Architect: Stanley Saitowitz | Natoma Architects, Inc.
Client: YBL LLC./ Ed Tansev
Completion date: 2002
Building area: 400,000 sq. ft. (37,161 sq. m)
Project team: Stanley Saitowitz, Michael Luke, John Winder, Naomi De Graff, Daishi Yoshimoto, Eric Staten
Collaborators:
Structural: Watry Design Group
MEP/security: design build
Acoustical: Charles M. Salter Associates Inc.
General contactor: Pankow Residential Builders
Project budget: $40,000,000

Tampa Museum of Art
Location: Tampa, Florida, USA
Architect: Stanley Saitowitz | Natoma Architects, Inc.
Client: City of Tampa
Completion date: 2010
Building area: 66,000 sq. ft. (6,132 sq. m)
Project team: Stanley Saitowitz, Neil Kaye, Markus Bischoff, John Winder
Collaborators
Structural: Walter P. Moore and Associates, Inc.
MEP/security: TLC Engineering for Architecture
Civil: Wilson Miller, Inc.
Lighting: ARUP Lighting Division
Acoustical: Siebein Associates, Inc.
General contactor: Skanska USA Building
Project budget: $26,000,000

Brigitte Shim and Howard Sutcliffe

Moorelands Camp Dining Hall
Location: Lake Kawagama, Haliburton, Ontario, Canada
Architects: Shim–Sutcliffe Architects
Client: Moorelands Community Services
Completion date: 2002
Building area: 6,809 sq. ft. (633 sq. m)
Project Architect: Jason Emery Groen
General Contractor: Gord McLean and crew assisted by Barry Chumbly
Structural Engineer: Atkins + Van Groll Inc.

Harrison Island Camp
Location: Georgian Bay, Ontario, Canada
Architect: Shim–Sutcliffe Architects
Client: Brigitte Shim and Howard Sutcliffe
Completion date: 2010
Building Area: 1,000 sq. ft. (93 sq. m)
General Contractor: Marshallbuilt
Sub-contractor: Two Degrees North–millwork, Tremonte Manufacturing–steel fabrication
Structural Engineer: David Bowick, Blackwell Bowick Partnership

Craven Road Studio
Location: Toronto, Ontario, Canada
Architect: Shim–Sutcliffe Architects
Client: Robert Hill
Completion date: 2006
Building Area: 550 sq. ft. (51 sq. m)
Project Architect: Michael Goorevich
General Contractor: Derek Nicholson Incorporated
Structural Engineer: David Bowick, Blackwell Bowick Partnership

Bet Ha'am Synagogue
Location: Portland, Maine
Architects: Shim–Sutcliffe Architects
Client: Jeremy Moser, Chair of Building Committee, Congregation Bet Ha'am
Completion date: 2007
Building Area: 11,500 sq. ft. (1,068 sq. m)
Project Architect: Olga Pushkar
General Contractor: Wright-Ryan Construction, Inc.
Structural Engineer: Blackwell Bowick Partnership Ltd. and L&L Structural Engineering Services Inc.

Island House
Location: Howe Island, St. Lawrence River, Ontario, Canada
Architect: Shim–Sutcliffe Architects
Client: Kevin and Carol Reilly
Completion date: 2001
Building area: 2,090 sq. ft. (194 sq. m)
Project team: Donald Chong, Jason Emery-Groen, John O'Connor
General Contractor: Peabody and Sheedy Construction
Structural Engineer: David Bowick, Blackwell Bowick Partnership

The Integral House
Location: Toronto, Ontario, Canada
Architect: Shim–Sutcliffe Architects
Client: Dr. James Stewart
Completion date: 2009
Building area: 15,000 sq. ft. (1,394 sq. m)
Project Architect: Betsy Williamson with project team, including Andrew Hart, Denise Haradem, Mike Goorevich, Kyra Clarkson
General Contractor: Eisner-Murray Developments Inc., Vic Furgiuele–site supervisor
Structural Engineer: David Bowick, Blackwell Bowick Partnership

Rick Joy

Desert Nomad House
Location: Tucson, Arizona, USA
Architects: Rick Joy, Chelsea Grassinger, Andy Tinucci, Franz Buhler, Cade Hayes
Client: Walter Cecil
Completion date: 2005
Building area: 1,500 sq. ft. (139 sq. m)
General Contractor: Rick Joy Architects
Structural Engineer: S.W. Engineering Structural

400 Rubio Avenue Studio
Location: Tucson, Arizona, USA
Architects: Rick Joy, Andy Tinucci, Chelsea Grassinger
Client: Rick Joy Architects
Completion date: 1999
Building Area Studio: 1400 sq. ft. (130 sq. m), Courtyard 700 sq. ft. (65 sq. m)
General Contractor: Rick Joy Architects
Structural Engineer: S.W. Engineering Structural

Adobe Canyon House
Location: Patagonia, Arizona, USA
Architects: Rick Joy, Mark Mishmash, Cade Hayes
Client: Neil Moss + Joan Godrich
Completion date: 2005
Building Area: 1,100 sq. ft. (102 sq. m)
General Contractor: Rick Joy Architects

Amangiri Resort
Location: Canyon Point, Utah, USA
Architects: 1-10 Studio: Marwan Al-Sayed Architect, Wendell Burnette Architects, Rick Joy Architects
Client: Aman Resorts
Completion date: 2009
Building area: 73,000 sq. ft. (6,782 sq. m)
Collaborators: Michael Boucher Landscape Architecture, Ljusarkitektur P & Ö AB Stockholm Lighting Design
General Contractor: Oakland Construction
Structural Engineer: Harris Engineering

Woodstock Farm
Location: Woodstock, Vermont, USA
Architects Team: Rick Joy, Dale Rush, Claudia Valent, Madeline Gradillas, Philip Neher, Nicolas Norero, Louise Girling, Hubert d'Autremont, James Barnfield
Clients: Dione and Paul Palandjian
Completion date: 2008
Building area: House 3,890 sq. ft. (361 sq. m), Main Barn 3,375 sq. ft. (314 sq. m), Barn Loft 2,250 sq. ft. (209 sq. m)
Collaborators: Michael Boucher Landscape Architecture, Ljusarkitektur P & Ö AB Stockholm Lighting Design
General Contractor: Colby & Tobiason
Structural Engineer: Harris Engineering

John and Patricia Patkau

Strawberry Vale School
Location: Victoria, British Columbia, Canada
Architect: Patkau Architects Inc
Client: Greater Victoria School District
Dates: 1992–1995
Project Team: Grace Cheung, Michael Cunningham, Michael Kothke, Timothy Newton, John Patkau, Patricia Patkau, David Shone, Peter Suter, Allan Teramura, John Wall, Jacqueline Wang
Model Makers: Tim Newton, John Wall
Photographer: James Dow
Project Architect: Michael Cunningham/David Shone
Consultants: C.Y. Loh Associates Ltd., structural engineer; D.W. Thomson Consultants Ltd., mechanical engineer; Reid Crowther & Partners Ltd., electrical engineer; Duncan & Associates Engineering Ltd., civil engineer; Thurber Engineering Ltd., geotechnical engineer; Moura Quayle/Lanark Consultants Ltd., landscape architect; Gage-Babcock & Associates, fire protection consultant; BTY Group, costing consultant; Barron Kennedy Lyzun & Associates Ltd., acoustics consultant; Environmental Research Group University of British Columbia School of Architecture, materials consultant; Susan Morris Specifications, specifications consultant; Vaitkunas Design Inc., signage consultant
Contractor: JCR Construction
Awards: Canadian Architect Award, 1994
Progressive Architecture Award, 1995
Governor General's Medal, 2002
Area: 35,416 sq. ft. (3,290 sq. m)
Construction Cost: $5,540,000
Sustainability: LEED Certification

Grande Bibliothèque du Québec, Canada
Location: Montreal, Québec
Architect: Patkau Architects/Croft Pelletier/Menkès Shooner Dagenais architectes associés
Competition: Patkau Architects/Croft Pelletier/Gilles Guité architectes
Client: Bibliothèque nationale du Québec
Dates: 2000–2005
Project Team: Laura Arpiainen, Greg Boothroyd, Stephan Chevalier, Michael Cunningham (Project Architect), Dominique Dumais, Michael Elkan, Samantha Hayes, John Patkau, Patricia Patkau, Peter Suter, Craig Simms, Nick Sully
Competition Team: Vaughn Berg, Eric Boelling, Greg Boothroyd, Judy Cheung, Marie-Chantal Croft, Michael Cunningham, Gilles Guité, Samantha Hayes, Timothy Newton, Patrick O'Sullivan, John Patkau, Patricia Patkau, Eric Pelletier, Kathleen Robertson, David Shone, Cédéanne Simard, Craig Simms, Kristine Solberg, Peter Suter, Nick Sully

Model Makers: Thomas Lee, Imke Maron, Christian Schulte, Craig Simms, Tokimi Ota, Jan Rasche, Eric Roth
Photographers: James Dow, Patkau Architects Inc
Consultants: Gilles Guité Architecte, consulting architect; Jodoin Lamarre Pratte et Associés Architectes, architectural support; Regroupement Nicolet Chartrand Knoll Limitée/Les Consultants Géniplus Inc., structural engineer; Le Consortium Bouthillette, Pariseau & Associés Inc./Groupe HBA Experts-Conseils Inc., mechanical/electrical engineer; NBBJ, lighting consultant; Legault Davidson, acoustics consultant; Scenoplus, theater consultants; KJA Inc., elevators consultant; Technorm Inc., code consultant; Scheme Consultants, landscape architect, laboratory consultant, Inspec Sol
Contractor: Hervé Pomerleau-builder
Awards: Winning Submission, International Design Competition 2000
Area: 573,875 sq. ft. (53,315 sq. m)
Construction Cost: $71,000,000
Sustainability: LEED Certification

Linear House
Location: Salt Spring Island, British Columbia, Canada
Architect: Patkau Architects Inc
Dates: 2006–2009
Project Team: Greg Boothroyd, Christina Gray, Steffen Knab, Hiro Kurozumi, Renee Martin, John Patkau, Patricia Patkau, Peter Suter (Project Architect)
Consultants
Structural: Read Jones Christoffersen Ltd.
Building Envelope: Spratt Emanuel Engineering Ltd.
Contractor: Gordon Speed, G-Speed Construction Ltd.
Area: 3,500 sq. ft. (325 sq. m)

Steven Holl

School of Art and Art History, University of Iowa
Location: Iowa City, Iowa, USA
Date: 2006
Client: University of Iowa
Architect: Steven Holl Architects, Steven Holl, Chris McVoy, Martin Cox (design architect) Martin Cox (associate in charge) Li Hu, Gabriela Barman-Kraemer (project architect) Arnault Biou, Regina Chow, Elissavet Chryssochoides, Hideki Hirahara, Brian Melcher, Chris Otterbine, Susi Sanchez, Irene Vogt, Urs Vogt (project team)
Local architect: Herbert Lewis Kruse Blunck Architecture
Structural engineer: Guy Nordenson and Associates
Associate structural engineer: Structural Engineering Associates
Mechanical engineer: Alvine & Associates
Curtain wall consultant: WJ Higgins & Co.
Civil engineer: Shive-Hattery
General contractor: Larson Construction
Program: Art and art history building, including facilities for sculpture, painting, printmaking, graduate studios, administrative offices, gallery, and library
Cost: $16,100,000
Area: 70,000 sq. ft. (6,503 sq. m)

Nelson-Atkins Museum of Art
Location: Kansas City, Missouri, USA
Client: Nelson-Atkins Museum of Art
Date: 2007
Architect: Steven Holl Architects, Steven Holl, Chris McVoy (design architect), Chris McVoy (partner in charge), Martin Cox, Richard Tobias (project architect), Masao Akiyoshi, Gabriela Barman-Kraemer, Matthias Blass, Molly Blieden, Elissavet Chryssochoides, Robert Edmonds, Simone Giostra, Annette Goderbauer, Mimi Hoang, Makram El-Kadi, Edward Lalonde, Li Hu, Justin Korhammer, Linda Lee, Fabian Llonch, Stephen O'Dell, Irene Vogt, Urs Vogt, Christian Wassmann (project team)
Local architect: BNIM Architects
Structural engineer: Guy Nordenson and Associates
Associate structural engineer: Structural Engineering Associates
Mechanical engineer: Ove Arup & Partners, W.L. Cassell & Associates
Glass consultant: R.A. Heintges & Associates
Lighting consultant: Renfro Design Group
Landscape architect: Gould Evans Goodman Associates
Program: museum addition and renovation
Project type: competition
Cost: $85,900,000
Area: 165,000 sq. ft. (15,329 sq. m)

Queens Community Library
Location: Queens, New York, USA
Client: Queens Library, New York City Department of Design and Construction
Estimated Completion Date: 2012
Architect: Steven Holl Architects, Steven Holl, Chris McVoy (design architects), Olaf Schmidt (associate in charge), Filipe Taboada (project architect), Rychiee Espinosa, Jeanne Wellinger (project team)
Engineer: Robert Silman Associates, ICOR Associates
Program: Library with adult reading collection, children's area, teen area, cybercenter, conference room and outdoor amphitheater
Project type: competition (first prize)
Area: 21,000 sq. ft. (1,951 sq. m)

Image Credits

"Architecture and Continuity: North American Architecture 1990–2010"
p. 6: © Kooho Jung
p. 15: © Willi Kunz

Stanley Saitowitz, "Simplicity and Synthesis"
p. 18 top: Flickr
pp. 18 bottom–21 © Stanley Saitowitz | Natoma Architects, Inc.
pp. 22–23: © Tim Griffith
p. 25 © Stanley Saitowitz | Natoma Architects, Inc.
p. 26 top: © Stanley Saitowitz | Natoma Architects, Inc.;
p. 26 bottom: © Tim Griffith
p. 27 top: © Liz McBee
p. 27 bottom © Tim Griffith
p. 28: © Stanley Saitowitz | Natoma Architects, Inc.
p. 29: © Tim Griffith
pp. 31–33: © Richard Barnes
p. 34 top: © Walter P Moore
p. 34 bottom: © Stanley Saitowitz | Natoma Architects, Inc.
pp. 35–37: © Richard Barnes

Brigitte Shim and Howard Sutcliffe, "The Craft of Place"
pp. 40–43: © Shim-Sutcliffe Architects Inc
p. 44: © Michael Awad
p. 45 top: © Shim-Sutcliffe Architects Inc
p. 45 bottom: © James Dow
pp. 47–48: © Shim-Sutcliffe Architects Inc
p. 49: © Finn O'Hara
p. 50: © Bob Gundu
pp. 51–52 top: © Shim-Sutcliffe Architects Inc
p. 52 bottom: © James Dow
p. 53 top: © Shim-Sutcliffe Architects Inc
p. 53 bottom: © James Dow
pp. 54–55: © Shim-Sutcliffe Architects Inc
p. 56: © James Dow
pp. 57–59 top: © Shim-Sutcliffe Architects Inc
p. 59 bottom: © Ed Burtynsky
pp. 60–61: © James Dow
p. 63 top: © Bob Gundu
p. 63 bottom: © Ed Burtynsky.

Rick Joy, "Proximity and Distance"
p. 67: © Rick Joy Architects
pp. 68–69: © Jeff Goldberg/Esto
pp. 70–72: © Rick Joy Architects
p. 73 top: © Rick Joy Architects
p. 73 bottom: © Rick Joy Architects
p. 74: © Joe Fletcher
p. 75 top: © Rick Joy Architects + I-10 Studio
p. 75 bottom: © Rick Joy Architects
pp. 76–77: © Joe Fletcher
p. 78: © Jean-Luc Laloux
p. 79 top: © Rick Joy Architects
p. 79 bottom: © Jean-Luc Laloux

John and Patricia Patkau, "The Structure of Relationships"
p. 82: © James Dow
p. 83–85: © Patkau Architects Inc
pp. 86–90: © James Dow
p. 91: © Bernard Fougères/Bibliothèque Nationale du Québec
p. 93: © Patkau Architects Inc
p. 94 top: © Bernard Fougères/Bibliothèque Nationale du Québec
pp. 94 middle–95: © James Dow
pp. 96–99 top: © Patkau Architects Inc
p. 99 middle: © James Dow
p. 99 bottom: © Patkau Architects Inc
p. 101 top: © James Dow
p. 101 bottom: © Patkau Architects Inc
p. 103: © Patkau Architects Inc
pp. 102–104: © James Dow

Steven Holl, "Rule and Exception"
pp. 108–110 top: © Steven Holl Architects
p. 110 bottom: © Christian Richters
p. 111 top: © Steven Holl Architects
p. 111 bottom: © Andy Ryan
pp. 112–113: © Christian Richters
p. 115 top: © Steven Holl Architects
p. 115 bottom: © Roland Halbe
p. 116 top: © Steven Holl Architects
p. 116 bottom: © Andy Ryan
p. 117 top: © Roland Halbe
pp. 117 bottom–118 top: © Steven Holl Architects
p. 118 bottom: © Andy Ryan
pp. 120–121: © Roland Halbe
pp. 123–127: © Steven Holl Architects
pp. 128–129: © Steven Holl Architects

Further reading

Stanley Saitowitz | Natoma Architects Inc.

Michael Bell and Craig Buckley eds., *Solid States: Concrete in Transition,* (New York: Princeton Architectural Press, 2010).

Hilary French, *Key Urban Housing of the Twentieth Century: Plans, Sections, and Elevations,* (London: Laurence King Publishing, 2008).

Mitchell Schwarzer, *San Francisco: Architecture of the San Francisco Bay Area: A History and Guide,* (San Francisco: William Stout Publishers, 2007).

Stanley Saitowitz, *Stanley Saitowitz | Natoma Architects Inc.: Buildings and Projects,* (New York: Monacelli Press, 2005).

Edwin Heathcote, *Monument Builders: Modern Architecture and Death,* (Chichester, West Sussex: Academy Editions, 1999).

Stanley Saitowitz, *Architecture at Rice 33,* Michael Bell, ed., (New York: Princeton Architectural Press, 1997).

George Wagner ed., *Stanley Saitowitz: A House in the Transvaal,* (New York: Princeton Architectural Press, 1995).

Shim-Sutcliffe Architects

Marco Atzori, "Dwell-How; In the Light of the Given. A Continuous Timeline in Architecture," *C3 Magazine* 319 (2011), 72–89.

Ian Chodikoff, "Governor General's Awards 2010: Corkin Gallery, Ravine Guest House, Craven Road Studio," *Canadian Architect* 55 (2010), 22–23, 24–25, 28–29.

Elke Krasny, "Integral House, Toronto, Kanada – Mehr Als Ein Haus," *Architektur Aktuell* 361 (2010), 110–120.

"Living in, Looking Out. Shim-Sutcliffe Architects, The Integral House," *A+U Architecture and Urbanism* 477 (2010), 26–33.

Clifford Pearson, "A Surround Sound," *Architectural Record* 198 (2010), 67–71.

Michael Webb, "Highlights: Integral House– Toronto, Canada, Shim-Sutcliffe Architects," *The Plan* 46 (2010), 52–66.

Sara Lin, "An 'Accordion' of Wood and Glass," *Wall Street Journal–The Home Front* (April 3, 2009).

Phaidon, eds., *10 × 10/3,* (London: Phaidon Press Limited, 2009).

"Dwelling and the Land: Shim-Sutcliffe Architects, House on Hurricane Lake," *A+U Architecture and Urbanism* 458 (2008), 30–41.

Rick Joy Architects

Rick Joy: Interludes, DVD, Directed by Muffie Dunn, (New York: Checkerboard Foundation, Inc. 2009).

Cathleen McGuigan, "A Certain Sense of Calm," *Newsweek* (Special Double Issue, July 2, 2007/ July 9, 2007), 52–60.

Mikko Heikkinen, ed., "Elephant & Butterfly," *Publication for the 9th Alvar Aalto Symposium,* (Finland: Alvar Aalto Academy, 2004), 25–40.

Alison Beard, "Building on the Rhythms of Living," *Financial Times,* October 30, 2004.

Rick Joy, *Desert Works,* (New York: Princeton Architectural Press, 2002).

Patkau Architects

Patkau Architects, (New York: The Monacelli Press, 2006).

Lisa Rochon, "The Patkaus' Art of Architecture," *Up North: Where Canada's Architecture Meets the Land,* (Toronto, Ontario: Key Porter Books, 2005), 267–277.

Phaidon, eds., *The Phaidon Atlas of Contemporary World Architecture,* (London: Phaidon, 2004).

Annette LeCuyer, *Radical Tectonics,* (London: Thames and Hudson, 2001), 90–120.

John Patkau, *Material Differences, Matter and Mind in Architecture,* (Hämeenlinna: Alvar Aalto Foundation, 2000), 84–99.

Patricia Patkau, "Technology, Lecture, Place and Architecture," *The Jerusalem Seminar in Architecture,* Kenneth Frampton, ed., (New York: Rizzoli International Publications Inc, 1998), 94–111.

Patkau Architects, (Barcelona: Gustavo Gili, 1997).

Laura Arpiainen, "Conversation with John Patkau," *Arkkitehti* (February/March 1995), 38–43.

Patkau Architects, *The 1995 John Dinkeloo Memorial Lecture,* Annette W. LeCuyer, ed., (Ann Arbor: The University of Michigan, 1995).

Steven Holl Architects

Steven Holl, *Horizontal Skyscraper,* (San Francisco: William Stout Publishers, 2011).

Steven Holl, Sanford Kwinter and Jordi Safont-tria, *Color Light Time,* (Zurich: Lars Müller Publishers, 2011).

Steven Holl, *Scale: An Architect's Sketch Book,* (Zurich: Lars Müller Publishers, 2011).

Steven Holl, *Pamphlet Architecture* 11–20, (New York: Princeton Architectural Press, 2011).

Steven Holl, *Urbanisms: Working With Doubt,* (New York: Princeton Architectural Press, 2009).

Jeffrey Kipnis, *Stone & Feather: Steven Holl Architects/The Nelson Atkins Museum Expansion,* (London: Prestel, 2007).

Steven Holl, *House: Black Swan Theory,* (New York: Princeton Architectural Press, 2007).

Steven Holl, Juhani Pallasmaa and Alberto Perez-Gomez, *Questions of Perception,* (San Francisco: William Stout Publishers, 2007).

Steven Holl, *Architecture Spoken,* (New York: Rizzoli, 2007).

Steven Holl, *Parallax,* (New York: Princeton Architectural Press, 2000).

All dimensions indicated in the plans are in meters.

Acknowledgments

The making of this book would not have been possible without the help of many people. In the first instance, the author wishes to thank Dean Mark Wigley and Benjamin Prosky without whose prompting and patronage none of this would have happened. Further to this he would like to thank the practices who contributed to the symposium and the subsequent anthology; namely, Stanley Saitowitz, Brigitte Shim and Howard Sutcliffe, Rick Joy, John and Patricia Patkau, and Steven Holl. Last, but not least, the author wishes to thank Lars Müller, along with Craig Buckley and Atreyee Ghosh, both of whom played a crucial editorial role in the Office of Publications at the Graduate School of Architecture, Planning, and Preservation.

Five North American Architects
An Anthology by Kenneth Frampton
In cooperation with GSAPP, Columbia University

Editor: Kenneth Frampton
Director of Publications, GSAPP: Craig Buckley
Design: Integral Lars Müller
Copyediting: Stephanie Salomon
Prepress: Photolitho AG, Gossau ZH
Printing and binding: Kösel, Altusried-Krugzell, Germany
Paper: LuxoArt Samt, 135 g/m²

This publication is the first in a series which will be devoted to the annual Kenneth Frampton Endowed Lecture. The Graduate School of Architecture, Planning, and Preservation thanks the donors whose generosity has enabled both the annual lecture and its publication.

Lars Müller Publishers
Zurich, Switzerland
www.lars-mueller-publishers.com

ISBN 978-3-03778-256-9

Printed in Germany